# THE SPIRIT OF ONE EARTH

# THE SPIRIT OF ONE EARTH

## Reflections on Teilhard de Chardin and Global Spirituality

by

### URSULA KING

A NEW ERA BOOK

Paragon House
New York

Published by Paragon House
90 Fifth Avenue
New York, NY 10011

**Library of Congress Cataloging-in-Publication Data**

King, Ursula.
     The spirit of one earth: reflections on Teilhard de Chardin and global
spirituality / by Ursula King.
        p.    cm.
     ISBN 0-913757-93-4
     1. Teilhard de Chardin, Pierre—Views on religion.    2. Religion—
History—20th century.    3.  Spirituality—History of doctrines—20th century.
4.  Mysticism—History—20th century.    I. Title.
B2430.T374K54 1988
291'.092'4—dc19                                                           88-9758
                                                                                       CIP

# Acknowledgments

Earlier versions of different chapters in this book were first published as articles, and the permission of editors to reprint this material is gratefully acknowledged. Chapter 1 first appeared in *The Teilhard Review*, London (vol. 19, 1984), as did chapters 3 and 8 (vol. 11, 1976), chapter 9 (vol. 10, 1975), and chapter 10 (vol. 9, 1974). Chapter 2 was published in *Social Action*, New Delhi (vol. 20, 1970), chapter 6 in *Religious Studies*, Cambridge (vol. 7, 1971), and chapter 7 in *World Faiths*, London (no. 106, 1978). The ideas in chapter 4 were first developed for a lecture given at the Teilhard de Chardin Centenary Conference, University of Leeds, 1981, and then revised for a symposium edited by J. Duerlinger, *Ultimate Reality and Spiritual Discipline*, New York: Paragon House, 1984. Some sections of chapter 5 incorporate ideas first presented in "Teilhard de Chardin's Interpretation of Mysticism," *Sciences Religieuses/Studies in Religion*, Waterloo/Ontario (vol. 8, 1979).

This book is dedicated to the memory of the Reverend Père Paul Henry, S.J. (1906-1984), who first introduced me to the ideas of Teilhard de Chardin and thereby greatly enlarged my vision of the world and the life of the spirit within it. These ideas have been a lasting inspiration for both my personal life and daily work, as they continue to be for many other people around the globe.

# Contents

Introduction: Global Spirituality and Teilhard de Chardin  1

Part I
Reflections on Spirituality and Society

1 Science and Mysticism
   Teilhard de Chardin and Religious Thought Today  15

2 Socialization and the Future of Humankind  29

3 The One and the Many
   Religious Perspectives on the Individual and
   Community in Contemporary Culture  45

4 The Phenomenon of Spirituality  65

5 Mysticism and Contemporary Society  83

Part II
Reflections on Interreligious Dialogue and Convergence

6 Religion and the Future
  Teilhard de Chardin's Thought as Contribution
  to Interreligious Dialogue                                101

7 Exploring Convergence
  The Contribution of World Faiths                          119

8 Teilhard's Association with
  the World Congress of Faiths, 1947-1950                    135

9 Teilhard's Comparison of Western
  and Eastern Mysticism                                     147

10 Aurobindo's and Teilhard's Vision of the
   Future of Humankind                                      165


Conclusion: Love—The Spirit of One Earth                    175


Notes                                                       185

## Introduction

# Global Spirituality and Teilhard de Chardin

We live in a world where more and more people are wondering where we are going. Will the earth and humankind have a future at all? Our spaceship earth appears to be an ever-shrinking globe beset by fast change, turmoil, and strife; our mutual interdependencies are so intricate that many problems and actions can only be handled globally. This is first of all true of material development, whether it concerns food production or distribution, the organization of work and leisure, or questions of health and international security. But a global context is equally required for education and scientific research, for the flowering of art, the use of the imagination, for matters of morality, ethics, and religion, and for questions of spiritual well-being.

People today are also becoming more aware of the need for a global spirituality. We are now learning to look at the religious heritage of humankind from a new, global perspective and discover that this heritage is one of the most valuable resources for the whole of humanity at a time of critical reflection and profound change. The French Jesuit scientist and mystic Pierre Teilhard de Chardin (1881-1955) wrote on many questions of spirituality and mysticism in a very moving, challenging, and thought-provoking way. Although he did not use the recently coined term "global spirituality," he nonetheless possessed the vison to which this expression points. His vocabulary was often different from ours, but his intuitions and thoughts are intimately connected with what we are urgently seeking and most in need of today.

What is this spirituality we are seeking? And in what sense is it global?

The word *spirituality* has been given so many different definitions that it would be impossible to list one that would apply equally to all the different spiritual schools and practices. For some, spirituality simply means our relationship to God. For others, it represents a deep existential commitment to a transcendent dimension within and beyond life, an experience of the powerful presence of the spirit. Spirituality is not a static given but can be understood as a dynamic process of transformation and growth, an integral part of human development toward maturity, in both an individual and collective sense. Spirituality has also been described as "an exploration into what is involved in becoming human" or as "an attempt to grow in sensitivity to self, to others, to non-human creation and to God who is within and beyond this totality."[1] Thus understood, spirituality is linked to the experience of freedom, creativity, commitment, and value. All these descriptions show that spirituality must not be perceived as something apart from life, or simply added on to it. Rather, it is a quality of experience, intuition, reflection, and being which permeates all human activities. The whole of life can be seen as being related to spiritual practice. Spirituality then concerns the heart of human existence, and its practice is linked to the use of our imagination as a faculty for seeing more deeply into the ground and meaning of things and experiences.

But what is meant by "global spirituality"? Initially, spirituality is both personal and collective; but it is global in the sense that it now has to be developed in a crosscultural context, as created by the contemporary political, social, and cultural realities of our globe. These realities invite us to understand and practice spirituality in a pluralistic perspective which implies the discovery that the different faiths and their distinct messages become newly meaningful in their new togetherness on the globe. The different religious traditons have been diffused and transplanted from their place of origin to new cultures and regions. Many more members of different faiths have an opportunity to come into contact with and learn from each other, and that includes learning to accept their differences. Instead of encountering each other in hatred and strife, we have to learn to give and receive from each other in openness and respect. Such learning is especially involved in the experiential process of *interreligious dialogue* between members of different faiths. It also occurs through *intrareligious* dialogue within the heart of each person and within the different communities who have to critically reflect on their own faith experience in the light of that of others.

But the word *global* does not refer only to an experience of the present. It also encompasses the past, for we are becoming increasingly aware of the history of humankind, including its religious history, as one. The numerous spiritual schools and personalities which have existed throughout history around the globe provide us with extraordinary resources for contemporary religious awareness. When we speak of global spirituality, we think of a dimension that cuts across the present, extends back into the deep past, and reaches out toward the future to feed and strengthen the human spirit on its journey through time and space.

We also think of global spirituality in yet another sense: today spirituality has become an issue for *all* of humanity, not just for a select group of religiously-minded people for whom spirituality happens to be a special area of interest. At the present critical time in human history we have to pay particular attention to the deep need for spiritual well-being beyond the existing physical, mental, and moral needs of humankind. We have to ask ourselves: will questions of spiritual development one day become an integral part of our efforts to ensure global development towards peace and justice? What efforts do we at present devote toward developing the inner resources of human beings, their imagination, mind and heart, their power to love, care, and be compassionate as well as peaceful and happy? These are serious questions at the level of global development; they have to be faced by secular institutions and the whole of society, for they cannot be solved by religious institutions alone. The most thought-provoking reflections on the place of spirituality in secular society are found in the book *New Genesis – Shaping a Global Spirituality* by the Assistant Secretary General of the United Nations, Robert Muller, who, through working for many years for what is perhaps the largest secular institution in the world, has come to realize the urgent need for spiritual development among humankind today.[2]

There is some doubt whether religion, as traditionally understood, has a future today, given the increasing growth of secularization around the world. A more basic question, however, is: Has our world a future? Or what future is there for humankind today? Given contemporary political and military developments, the answer to this question is far from certain and cannot be taken for granted. In any case, the future no longer simply arrives and is given, as it was in the past; it has to be willed and created in full consciousness of what is involved in our actions and what goals we want to aim for. Teilhard de Chardin wrote with extraordinary hope, perhaps more than most of us can muster today, but his hope was so extraordinary because he was aware of the great threat, the extreme vulnerability and precariousness of human beings who, at the present stage of development and consciousness, have to will a future and build a new earth – if they want to have a future worth having at all. Today's threat of the possibility of extinguishing humans as a species calls in a completely new way on all the powers of our imagination, our will, and our inner and outer resources.

For Teilhard, the future can be willed, constructed, and built if we can perceive and practice the right kind of religion and spirituality. For many people today the social, outward aspects of religion are less important than the personal, inward ones, as is evident from the importance assigned to religious experience, spirituality, and mysticism. While religion has lost much of its social significance, its public power and influence, particularly in the West, we can also observe a profound transformation of religious consciousness in new powers of religious sensitivity and perception. Looking around for resources to feed our thought and imagination, to strengthen our will to act, we ask ourselves: Can Teilhard de Chardin still speak to us today, in our search for global spirituality? He wrote during the first half of the twentieth century while we, near the close of its second half, are already fast approaching the threshold of the third millenium—a new age desperately in need of a new spirit.

It is true that Teilhard addressed a different readership and audience from that of today, often a specialized public with a training in and commitment to scientific research. Many of his thoughts were compressed into short reports and notes, not unlike those of a scientific memoir. Even many of his longer essays share a certain dryness of language, especially in their English translation. This often makes it difficult for people to capture the emotional intensity and visionary quality of Teilhard the mystic, who believed it was his vocation to extend people's capacity to see into the heart of things by sharing with them a larger vison of the world and the destiny of mankind. The vibrations of his mind and soul are more often sensed in his letters, diaries, and early mystical writings, which reverberate with a deeply experienced "sense of plenitude,"[3] a sense of wholeness and communion with the dynamic, life-giving powers of the spirit which animate all parts of the cosmos, all life, all our being.

In many ways Teilhard speaks strongly to our concerns today, but he is not as often heard or listened to as he deserves. One also needs to be patient and pay careful attention to the details of what he says if one wants to enter the large world of his vison and thought. He certainly wrote extensively on questions of spirituality, but not as traditionally understood. Also, he did not primarily speak as spiritual counselor to individuals (although he helped many personally in this way), but his major concern was to communicate a vision about the entire earth and its peoples, the immense process of movement at work in humankind in the making, the coming together of East and West into a new unity linked to the sense of one earth intimately related to what he called the development of a "terrestrial religious consciousness" or what we today would call a "global spirituality." Thus he spoke of "building the earth," of the need to redefine the spirit or create a new spirit within humankind, a spirit capable of creating a new human community through the powers of love rather than through the use of external force.

Teilhard considered the development of humankind since the dawn of time as intimately related to the rise of self-reflective, critical consciousness which, in turn, is linked to the development of greater self-awareness and inner centration in innumerable individual consciousnesses. This allows the powers of love and unification to increase, reaching outward through creating social transformation grounded in personal transformation. He often referred to this process as the emergence of a new mysticism of action and convergence. Such personal and social transformations are coming together in many contemporary liberation movements which are explicitly connected with the experience of consciousness-raising, whether in political freedom movements or in the women's liberation movement. Such an actively initiated process of changing consciousness, of making individuals and groups more intensely and critically aware, is directly linked with the rise of consciousness in humankind of which Teilhard speaks.

But in spite of this transformation, we are at a critical threshold where humanity has not yet found a common mind and spirit, a common sense of values on which it can agree and corporately act. In Teilhard's view and that of many other contemporary thinkers, this common sense is precisely what is needed to ensure the future of the human community at this moment. We need to develop the spirit of one earth, the spirit of global responsibility—a spirituality which can animate, develop, and strengthen the sense of being one human family with shared resources and mutual love for each other.

Before we say a little more about Teilhard's sense of the earth, let us mention some characteristics of his own spirituality, for his lived example can be a powerful inspiration too. Teilhard's mystical vision and experience were deeply Christian in origin and orientation, yet in much of what he saw, felt, and expressed, he broke through traditional boundaries and pointed to a vision global in intent. He lived a life deeply nourished and motivated by a dynamic Christian spirituality, a love of God and fellow beings, a love felt and sensed through all creation, whether human or divine.

I would like to single out three special marks of Teilhard's own spirituality. There is first of all the amazingly harmonious integration of an extraordinarily active life with contemplative/meditative modes of being over different periods of time. Linked to this rhythm was what he expressed in his spiritual classic, *The Divine Milieu* (1927), as "the divinisation of our activities and passivities." Teilhard truly was a great Christian mystic, a contemporary mystic in the best tradition of Christian mysticism, but also a mystic in search of a new mystical way, a new spirituality open to the rhythm of the world and deeply involved with its development.

A second aspect of his spirituality is expressed by the description of himself as a "wanderer between different worlds." This relates to his experience of roving in mind and spirit among the worlds of the past, present, and future, and the worlds of science, religion, and mysticism. He also moved in body and mind among different continents, cultures, and peoples in West and East. These "wanderings" give his thought a great deal of concreteness and elasticity as well as openness and strength. Even his most abstract musings are always rooted in the experience of the real. These wanderings are also a vivid contemporary expression of the old Christian theme of the pilgrim journeying through the world with and towards God. Teilhard made many journeys in his life and wherever he went, he asked what spiritual benefit and enrichment the very diverse experiences of his life gave him, what deeper spiritual meaning he could perceive in and through them. He saw in these experiences "the hands of God" which shaped his inner and outer life. Towards the end of his days he wrote to his friend and former collaborator, Père Leroy, that he felt he was now permanently living in the presence of God.

A third aspect of Teilhard's lived spirituality, an aspect that cannot be stressed enough, is his profound loyalty – his fundamental faithfulness to his vows, to his order, and to his church in spite of very many personal difficulties, doubts, and temptations. One can see in Teilhard a contemporary example of a "faithful servant of God" overcoming all trials in faith, hope, and love. He experienced anxiety, questioning, and hesitation, even shortly before his death, when he asked himself in the essay

"The Christic" whether the wonderful "diaphany" of the divine which had transfigured everything for him was perhaps no more than an illusion, a mirage of his own mind. He wondered whether his understanding of Christianity, his glorious vision of the cosmic Christ, were wrong, whether the flame of Christianity might become extinguished. After considering these questions, he replied with a definite "no" and continued to affirm his belief in the coherence of the Christian vision and the contagious power of love engendered by it.[4] This strength of faith, this Christian fortitude to which Teilhard's life gives such eloquent witness, can be a tremendous source of strength and inspiration for others. Quite a number of people have been encouraged and deepened in their faith by the personal example of his life, by his suffering, and by the intensity of devotion with which he continued to believe and love until the end. As his former Superior, Père d'Ouince, has said, when one examines the vicissitudes of his life, all the difficulties that conspired against him, one comes to the conclusion that in Teilhard we truly have "a prophet on trial."[5]

Through his worldwide travels in connection with his professional activities as a scientist, Teilhard concretely experienced the dimensions of the globe and the diversity of its populations and cultures. In 1931 he succinctly expressed his experience of the earth in the essay "The Spirit of the Earth,"[6] but the ideas of this essay go back to his early years of writing when, probably through meeting so many different human groups during the battles of the First World War and his travels to the East, he first voiced the desire to consider the destiny and interests of humanity as a whole by writing, not as a Frenchman or a Westerner, but as a "terrestrian."

In "The Spirit of the Earth," Teilhard affirms the primacy of the spirit in the universe, the evolution toward greater consciousness, as well as the "cosmic problem of action" in relationship to human unity and the development of scientific research. He asks, What is the future of the spirit of the earth? What is humankind's destiny? Darkness, total death, or a new life? He saw humanity undergoing a crisis of birth in which:

Everything depends on the prompt emergence of a soul which by merely appearing will come to organize, lighten and vitalize this mass of stagnant and confused matter. Now this soul, if it exists, can only be the "conspiration" of individuals, associating to *raise* the edifice of life *to a new stage.* The resources at our disposal today, the powers that we have released, *could not possibly be absorbed* by the narrow system of individual or national units which the architects of the human earth have hitherto used . . . *The age of nations has passed. Now, unless we wish to perish we must shake off our old prejudices and build the earth* . . . The more scientifically I regard the world, *the less can I see any possible biological future for it except the active consciousness of its unity.*[7]

Instead of thinking that humankind at the present stage of its development has no more need for religion, Teilhard stressed in this essay, as in others, that religion must grow and develop with the development of humankind. Only the spirit engendered by a transformed kind of religion can sustain the continuity and progress of life on earth. He speaks of a "redefinition" of the spirit, an emerging "new spirit" linked to the double transformation of a *new humanism* which discovers a sense of transcendence beyond this world, and a *renewed Christian faith and mysticism* which incorporates the values of this world in its own vision of faith.

Teilhard always emphasized the self-reflective nature of human knowledge, a consciousness that is self-critically aware of its own stage of development and therefore must consider the direction of its further growth and expansion. The development of consciousness is not only a mental occurrence; it affects all aspects of human life—feeling, emotion, imagination, and action. It is what Teilhard called the emergence and rise of the noosphere, of a global layer of thought and interaction. As such it has collective and individual, outward and inward, aspects. In one sense consciousness is linked to a depth dimension we call conscience, and to spiritual awareness. In our contemporary context the understanding of spirituality as a historical phenomenon is also gaining increasing importance for us today. By taking stock of how spirituality was understood and practiced in the past, by critically sifting our global heritage, we are helped to reflect on what direction spirituality can and will be taking from now on.

Over the last twenty years the interest in interreligious encounter and dialogue has helped to spread a greater awareness of the rich diversity of our global religious heritage. Such an awareness grows into vivid personal experience when people from different faiths take part in dialogue meetings or witness each other's worship at a grassroots level or in international gatherings as happened, for example, at the great gathering of the Assembly of World Religions in New Jersey in 1985.[8] Given the growing interest in spirituality, a number of programs and courses have been developed and many works on either historical or contemporary aspects of spirituality have been published. *The Study of Spirituality*, edited by Cheslyn Jones, Geoffrey Wainwright, and Edward Yarnold, S.J.[9] is a Christian ecumenical venture reflecting the wide range of the Christian spiritual heritage from its beginnings until today, with a brief acknowledgment of the spiritual resources of other religious traditions. On a much larger scale, we now have the new *Encyclopedia of World Spirituality*[10] which, in a series of twenty-five projected volumes, reflects the history of the religious quest in a global ecumenical perspective. In this large work, created by the collaborative effort of many authors, the movement of the spirit, both individually and collectively, throughout the history of humankind into the present, is traced. Spirituality is here seen as lived experience as well as reflection on such experience. This work also points to an emerging new discipline of global spirituality, providing a new focus for individual religious traditions through which they can see and reflect upon their own religious heritage in a larger context. As the general editor, Ewert Cousins, says in his preface to the series: ". . . it may well be that the meeting of spiritual paths – the assimilation not only of one's own spiritual heritage but that of the human community as a whole – is the distinctive spiritual journey of our time."[11]

When looking at the worldwide encounter of spiritualities in a global context, we should not leave Teilhard de Chardin's ideas unconsidered. Both his life and thought provide inspiring elements for developing global, crosscultural, and convergent perspectives on spirituality in modern society. His reflections on cultural and religious pluralism, on interreligious encounter between people from East and West, on the spirit of one earth, and on the need for a viable, action-oriented spirituality can illumine our thinking and direct our action in shaping the present and the future.

There are two important themes in Teilhard's approach to spirituality: one is concerned with the development of society at a global level, the future of the earth and humankind; the other considers the process of a convergence, the closer coming together of the human community and the energy resources available for this within our global religious heritage. The following essays, written over a number of years, address both these themes. Some of the essays discuss aspects of religion, spirituality, and mysticism in a wider context, while others look more closely at specific writings of Teilhard that have a bearing on his understanding of spirituality. Part I, entitled "Reflections on Spirituality and Society," explores how Teilhard relates the understanding of modern science to that of mysticism (chapter 1), how the future of humankind is dependent on a greater unification of the human community which enhances rather than negates personal growth (chapter 2), and how these perspectives on the personal and social—"The One and the Many"— have been given a varying degree of emphasis in different religious traditions (chapter 3). From early on Teilhard reflected on spirituality as a decisive element in the evolution of humanity. This reflection is particularly evident from an explicit essay on "The Phenomemon of Spirituality" (chapter 4) and from the emphasis placed on a new mysticism of action for the development of society (chapter 5).

Part II is concerned with "Reflections on Interreligious Dialogue and Convergence." It amplifies the reflections of the first part by considering Teilhard's thought on Eastern religions and interreligious encounter in an increasingly pluralistic world. Teilhard lived for more than twenty years in China and traveled widely in the East. His concern with the religious traditions and spiritual heritage of the East, as well as the parallels between his thought and that of the East, have been the subject of several studies,[12] but on the whole this aspect of Teilhard's work has made far less impact than other ideas. Thus it has not been given the attention it deserves, especially not in the discussions concerning theology, religion, and spirituality in a world context. Teilhard's thought on religion and the future can be examined in relationship to interreligious dialogue (chapter 6) while his notion of convergence is related to the special emphasis given to the contribution of world faiths to an emerging global civilization (chapter 7). Also little known is Teilhard's personal contact with and support for the work of the French branch of the World Congress of Faiths, for which he wrote several brief essays and addresses (chapter 8). Two of his essays, written fifteen years apart, make explicit comparisons between Western and Eastern mysticism (chapter 9). In spite of warranted criticisms, these essays still have something to say to us today. An intriguing parallel between Teilhard's thought and that of an Eastern thinker, Sri Aurobindo, is provided by their vision of the role of religion for the future of humankind (chapter 10). The conclusion takes up the theme of the spirit of one earth by considering *the* central focus of all of Teilhard's ideas on spirituality and mysticism: love and its power to transform the world and ourselves.

# Part I

# Reflections on Spirituality and Society

## *1*

# Science and Mysticism

Pierre Teilhard de Chardin was once described as "a thinker for all seasons." What can this thinker give us today? Can he still inspire and guide our own thinking? Can he speak to the religious search of our contemporaries in an age of change and turmoil, in an age when humankind is "in search of a soul," to quote Carl Gustav Jung or the Indian thinker Radhakrishnan or Teilhard himself?

Let us assess Teilhard's importance in relationship to science, religion, and mysticism by considering three questions:

1. What characterizes modern religious thought or, rather, the religious sensibility and temper of a scientific age such as ours?

2. What was Teilhard's approach to science, religion, and mysticism?

3. What is Teilhard's contribution to religious thought today, especially in the area of spirituality and mysticism?

### *1. The Characteristics of Modern Religious Thought and Experience*

Our age is so often described as an "age of unbelief," an age that seems to many spiritually impoverished, marked by a loss

*15*

of substance and transcendence and a disregard for the highest values. And yet to the discerning eye, there appear to be many signs of a sincere religious quest and a new spirituality emerging from within the secular. One must recognize the positive aspects of the very openness of the religious quest of many of our contemporaries, the doubt, the uncertainty, the groping, the willingness to experiment and to search for meaning. Thus it is not primarily abstract religious thought which is important today, but lived religious experience which is vital and is accepted as self-authenticating wherever it is found, within and without the traditional boundaries of relgous institutions.

This emphasis on experiment and experience—which is such a strong characteristic of our scientific approach to the external world—has also become more and more important for the worlds of our mind and soul. Contemporary religiosity is characterized by a great search for interiority and a new inwardness, a longing to explore our "inner space," which can provide a true counterweight to our dazzlingly dizzy scientific probes into outer space. This search for a contemplative depth-dimension within us responds to a great contemporary need to heal a hectic and disjointed outward life marked by overactivity, unrest, and much unsatisfactory superficiality in human relations.

But this hunger and thirst for interiority, for meditation, contemplation, and prayer are not the only characteristics of contemporary religious life. They are accompanied and matched by a search for a greater outward unification and unity at all levels, whether one thinks of the manifold experiments of living in new communities among the young and not so young, the increasing growth and flowering of genuine peace movements in both capitalist and socialist societies, or the dynamic thrust of the diverse liberation movements. They all possess implicit or explicit religious elements besides their social and political dimensions.

To think about religion and live it meaningfully today it is not enough to remain within the boundaries of traditional religiosity, whether they be those of church, temple, or mosque. The search for spirituality and transcendence in our age cannot find its sole answer in intense private devotions and an escapist religious life. Contemporary spirituality, if it is to have any effect on our lives, cannot flourish apart from the world, in cloisters, chapels, and churches, or whatever one's religious institution may be. It has to grow and live in the marketplace; it has to be a source of meaning for all of life and relate to our daily problems, our family and community, our science, our politics, our whole world as we scientifically explore and experience it today. This spirituality which we so much need as a true leaven and "bread of life" can only become a transforming agent of our world today, a true spirit to live and grow by, if it is nourished and nurtured within our secular institutions as well as within our traditional religious ones. Otherwise it will be impossible to create a world of peace and justice.

Many of our contemporaries hope, seek, and strive for such a spirituality, sometimes in the most unexpected ways and places. We are witnessing a profound transformation of contemporary religious consciousness. This process of transformation has deep roots in history, but it finds its most acute expression today in the search for a new, life-sustaining and world-related spirituality.

## 2. *Teilhard de Chardin's Approach to Science, Religion, and Mysticism*

But what has all this to do with Teilhard de Chardin, a man born over a century ago and dead for more than thirty years? Has this French priest and scientist, this explorer of the outer and inner world of human experience, still anything to say to our fast-changing societies, our huge problems, our religious needs of today? Some might answer, "very little," or "nothing at all," for they understand religion and spirituality as something unchanging and ever-abiding, something in total contrast to the values of the modern world. The assessment of Teilhard de Chardin within today's religious thought depends ultimately on one's approach to modern science; it also depends on how one judges these two areas—religion and science—as interrelated, and what importance one assigns to each for the whole of human life and experience.

The great discoveries and intellectual adventures of modern times have primarily been in the area of the sciences. They represent an ongoing, continuing quest for the exploration and understanding of the world around us and within us, the worlds of nature, of human beings, of societies.

The scientific quest can be described as a quest for more and more knowledge, a quest which forever expands our perception and experiences of the boundaries of the real, a quest which ultimately seeks the unity and interrelatedness of all knowledge. But like all human endeavors, the pursuit of science is characterized by a profound ambivalence. It has, so to speak, two faces. While the search for the unity of knowledge is its positive side, science, we all too well know, can have a dark, negative side; for its driving force can be the lust for power and domination, for exploitation and destruction. The power of analytical science is so crushingly great today that, if ruthlessly pursued to the limits of its possibilities and unchecked by any other force, it may soon pulverize us all into atomic fragments.

Teilhard de Chardin saw perhaps less of this dark shadow of modern science, its power for evil and destruction, than we perceive today. His own practice, praise, and love of science was undertaken from a position of responsibility, respect, and deep reverence, permeated by a religious spirit. Teilhard understood the scientific quest as a search for the unity of knowledge and saw it at its deepest level as closely related to the longing for union which finds expression in the religious and mystical quest.

The scientific and religious quests are the two great adventures of humanity involving all our imagination and creativity, opening to us further and further levels of reality and growth. It is in this spirit that Teilhard de Chardin published in 1939, a few months before the outbreak of World War II, an article on "The Mysticism of Science."[1] Here, as in many other essays, he makes clear how the pursuit of science, when seen from a sufficiently wide perspective and pursued in the right spirit, relates to religion and spirituality and becomes itself imbued with mysticism.

However, Teilhard also never tired of pointing out how our understanding of science is much too narrow, particularistic, and fragmentary. Its power of analysis must now be matched by attempts at synthesis, by a more holistic and global way of thinking. There is much to be criticized in modern science and we can see the depersonalizing effects of a narrowly understood scientific methodology and culture all around us. We have analyzed the physical-biological as well as the mental-psychic aspects of the human being, but we have not given anything like the same attention to the moral-spiritual needs of people in our presentation and practice of science.

This is where Teilhard saw everything from a wider, more universal, perspective and in need of transformation. Science and mysticism are not in opposition to each other, but ultimately interrelated. For him the rational and mystical are much closer than generally thought.

Teilhard de Chardin was both fundamentally modern and radically Christian. He was fundamentally modern in that he fully accepted and could only think within the categories of modern evolutionary science. He made full use of the empirical-analytical method of modern science but tried to overcome its limitations. He also had a deeply hopeful, positive outlook on the contemporary world in spite of all its problems.

In spite of the religious conservatism of his French aristocratic upbringing and background, Teilhard was a radical Christian because he had the courage to go back to the roots, to think afresh. He asked, What is central and distinctive about Christianity? How can the distinctive elements of Christianity creatively relate to the spiritual contributions of other world faiths? As he once wrote, others may praise God as pure spirit, but it was his particular vocation to sing God's praises as an incarnate being in all the fibers of this world.

Teilhard de Chardin lived and expressed a concrete spirituality, concrete in the sense that it was concerned with our concrete, real world, the world of matter, of flesh, of human and social development; concrete because he looked at the whole world and asked about the possibility of its future.

Teilhard's work and thought were deeply rooted in his religious and mystical experience. His life and writings are so closely intertwined that one cannot be understood without the other. The roots of his religious experience and vision go back to his childhood, where the love of nature was initially mediated by his father, whereas his religious life and knowledge of the mystics were kindled by his mother and later nourished by a wide reading of the mystics of all faiths. His inner development, bringing both the scientific and the mystical together, has been beautifully traced in his spiritual autobiography, *The Heart of Matter*.[2] There he describes the emergence of what he called his "cosmic sense," the desire and inclination to explore the world, the whole world beyond all frontiers. This cosmic sense was complemented by an equally ardent "christic sense," the mystical love and devotion, the desire and search for God seen by him in the universal and cosmic Christ, a powerful and radiant figure found in the hymns of St. Paul and the early Greek Fathers. But for Teilhard this cosmic Christ is now related to the whole world as we experience it today—the world which science makes us see in its infinite complexity, the world of nature and outer space, the world of many cultures, diverse races, and religions.

Teilhard's inner development was that of a mystic, but a mystic different from most in that his experience and thought about mysticism would have been impossible without the understanding and practice of modern science. Initially, his mystic experience was that of nature—the encounter with rocks, mountain, seas, and deserts—a rhapsodic love of the earth expressed in his early "Hymn to Matter" (1919),[3] matter which he saw as charged with the creative power of the spirit, as the "divine milieu" in which we move and have our being. He later used the image of the heart—the "heart of matter"—to express that all of reality has a center, a heart, a soul, a transcendent focus as well as an immanent, divine presence in the world. He thus could see the world as a cosmic sacrament where the divine, the energy of the spirit, shines through and is present as a truly dynamic, transformative power. For Teilhard, as for Gerard Manley Hopkins, the world was truly charged with the grandeur of God.

But Teilhard's mysticism was nourished not merely by the love of nature and the Christian sacraments. His mysticism emerged to the full in the fire of the trenches of the First World War, through the experience of the front and the sufferings of humanity. It was further shaped by the experience of the East and its peoples, especially through his long stay and travels in

China. It was there that he wrote his spiritual classics *The Mass on the World* (1923) and *The Divine Milieu* (1927), written "For those who love the world." It was there that he produced his best-known and perhaps most difficult book, *The Phenomenon of Man* (1938-40).

There always existed a close relationship between Teilhard's outer and inner development, his scientific pursuits and his creative religious writings. He always stressed the importance of "seeing" and thereby wanted to widen our perspective and vision. To see more, to see more clearly and distinctly, meant to him to become more, to live a fuller life. All his writings bear witness to the lifelong effort to communicate what he saw—a vision of unity and coherence, of the transformation of the world within and without, of the attainment of the spiritual in and through and beyond the material. He once said that the greatest success he could hope for was to have seen and shown others a new vision of the world.

In an essay entitled "My Fundamental Vision" (1984),[4] Teilhard explains in summary form how this vision is based on the data of modern science, their adequate interpretation in a wider context, and on a new understanding of mysticism. Teilhard's mysticism was directed towards the world and its development. He once described mysticism as "the science of Christ running through all things," but it was also "the only power capable of synthesizing the riches accumulated in other forms of human activity." The "new mysticism" of which he spoke so frequently meant for him the "sanctification of all human efforts, all sufferings, all joys." It was the pursuit of some spiritual Reality through and across all efforts of life which lead us to "the heart of the unique greatness of God."

Teilhard's entire life bears witness to the dynamic center of all religious life, that is, to the ardor of a mystic vision. This is the indispensable key for understanding his work and thought. But Teilhard was not only a religious man; he was also a great scientist. He qualified in geology, taught physics and chemistry, and excelled in paleontology, to which he devoted most of his working life. But the more he studied fossils and early human origins, the more his interest in the sciences of the past was changed into a fascination for the present and future of humankind. To make people see the implications of the past for the present development of one human family, to uncover the mysterious traces and pointers of evolution and set aflame the "sense of one earth" in his contemporaries, was Teilhard's great wish when he wrote *The Phenomenon of Man.* It is in the application of the dynamic categories of evolution, of the ideas of process and growth to religious thought, that Teilhard's science becomes tinged with mysticism and conveys a vision greater than what either traditional science or traditional religion can give. Thus Teilhard was both an ardent scientist and a mystic, a "scientist and seer," as Charles Raven so aptly described him in the title of his early biography.[5]

### 3. Teilhard de Chardin's Contribution to Religious Thought Today, Especially to Spirituality and Mysticism

Teilhard's approach to science was shaped by spiritual values and by the wisdom of mystical insight. But it was not spiritual romanticism, as some critics have maintained. He was ultimately a great realist, rooted in the grounds of the Real, but a Real which he understood to be so much vaster, stronger, and greater than most of us. Teilhard was really a pioneer of what is today called "new age thinking," one of the early observers of our planet Earth who clearly saw its need for a profound transformation, for an entirely new culture which cannot come about without a new spirituality. Changes at the surface are no longer enough. We need a transformation of our deepest structures, of our values, our social organization, our attitude to peace and war, to the distribution of our physical and spiritual resources, to the very use of science itself. We need a new spirituality which relates to the whole earth.

Already in the late thirties Teilhard reflected on the role of spirituality and pleaded for technicians and engineers of spiritual energy resources who can help to develop the sense of one world, of one human family. If we do not nourish the life of the spirit within us, both individually and collectively, we shall lose the zest and love for life, the will to work for a better life, for building up one world together in a spirit of love and unification rather than hatred and division. Teilhard was emphatic in saying that it is necessary for the religions themselves to change in order to meet the new needs of our world today; it is also necessary to develop a new morality and new ethics to deal with our global problems.

When Teilhard wrote about "The Mysticism of Science" (1939), he made it quite clear that science itself cannot be a substitute for true religion, as it so often was in the nineteenth century. But this "religion of science" was built on crude materialism and mechanistic conceptions of life which are almost dead today. Modern physics, modern biology, and the social sciences give us a much more subtle and complex picture of our world than the rationalistic approach of an earlier generation ever allowed for. With greater knowledge we also experience greater limits and perceive boundaries of genuine mystery which can make us truly humble and reverent. Thus Teilhard speaks about the need for a new mysticism and the place of a rightly understood religion in science.

While it is impossible to take up modern science without rethinking one's whole view of religion, it is equally important to see that the sciences fuel a new faith, a faith in the human being and the development of the world which Teilhard considers as closely related to faith in the spirit, in God. He sees in "our sacred pursuit of science," in our "modern mysticism of discovery," an energy of a fundamentally religious nature.[6] But ultimately this energy must be nourished and driven by the forces of love. Only then research becomes a work of worship and adoration.

Today Teilhard de Chardin is no longer alone in speaking about the need to introduce love into our practice of science. The Assistant Secretary General of the United Nations, Robert Muller, speaks extensively of this need in his book *New Genesis: Shaping a Global Spirituality*,[7] and his very practical suggestions in educating ourselves for spirituality in a global perspective are deeply influenced by Teilhard de Chardin. Muller once again emphasizes, as Teilhard and others have done, that the development of spirituality is colossally lagging behind our enormously impressive advances in science and technology and yet, like Teilhard, Muller also sees the development of science itself as part of the spiritual growth process at work within humankind.

The external forces of unification that press in upon us in the field of economics, politics, and world communications are by themselves not enough to create one world. The most powerful energy in bringing about a greater unity of mankind is the energy of love. Teilhard used to say that we must summon and harness the powers of love—the powers of an all-transforming spiritual energy—as we have harnessed the powers of wind and water, of atoms and genes, in order to build a future worth living, a future which will extend rather than diminish our capacity of being human.

Together with other critics of our age, Teilhard recognized that our modern Western culture is diseased with the cancer of rationality; it has been developed one-sidedly in an overly rationalistic, materialistic way, lacking the depth of feeling, the loving forces of the heart needed for all harmonious living. Teilhard wanted to bring the rational and mystical, the scientific and religious sides of our being together and he thereby created an inspiring vision. There is a telling anecdote about Teilhard which says that Descartes' famous statement "I think, therefore I am" was rephrased by the philosopher Blondel into "I will, therefore I am" and then expressed by Teilhard in the form "I love, therefore I am." This anecdote expresses more than any other what is of the greatest importance in his thought—how all our thinking and willing is naught without the powers of love.

Teilhard's major contribution to religious thought today lies primarily in the inspiring example of his life, and in the comprehensive range of his vision. His dedication as a scientist and priest and his loyal faithfulness to his church and order through all the vicissitudes and trials of his life make him a true Christian pilgrim of our age, a pilgrim with his roots deep in the past and his face turned to the future, with his arms wide open to embrace the whole world. He stepped far beyond the traditional boundaries of scientific and religious orthodoxies; his emphasis was always on lived experience rather than on abstract religious thought divorced from the realities of our daily world. Unlike many others, he could see the value of an open religious quest, of an inquiry into spiritual and mystical resources of the world religions, even if some may go astray in this quest.

We are always inspired by the example of others. Teilhard speaks to those who seek — who seek a larger vision, an action-oriented spirituality, a religion that can nourish all of human endeavor. As he himself wrote in 1949, for a vision to be convincing, it must communicate itself:

> What we need is not treatises or books, but men who will serve as examples, men . . . who will be passionately and *simultaneously* animated in both types of faith (that is, the faith in man and the faith in God, the faith in science and in religion) and so effect in themselves, *in one heart* the junction of the two mystical forces, and display . . . the realisation of the synthesis. We need men who are all the more convinced of the sacred value of human effort in that they are primarily interested in God.[8]

Many of our contemporaries have been inspired in their creative, scientific, or pastoral work by Teilhard's example of a lived faith, a concrete, practical spirituality that gives meaning to life, in us and in the universe.

Teilhard's thought on the role of religion in human development deserves much closer study than it has received so far. The whole development of what he calls "the phenomenon of man" from its earliest beginnings to today and beyond, is seen by him as animated by the forces of religion, the forces of the spirit, which are by no means outdated, but are more important today than ever. Central to the development of religion itself are for him a rightly understood spirituality and mysticism, most of all a mysticism of unification and greater unity, animated by the powers of love. Teilhard's well-known idea of the "noosphere" does not only refer to a growing layer of thought, a rise in conscious reflection and invention, surrounding the earth, but it also implies the idea of the growing union of souls, a sphere of true love, spreading around our globe.

Our deepest spiritual energy reserves are found in the religious heritage of humankind, and Teilhard felt that in spite of the diversity of our traditions, we have to pool our resources here, in the field of religions as elsewhere, and develop *meaningfully together*. His long experience of the East and its diverse religons made Teilhard sensitive to other religious worldviews, but he saw the further evolution of religion itself on a pattern of convergence, through the unification of the aims of the different faiths. Teilhard supported all efforts for greater unity. It is little known that he was one of the early supporters of the World Congress of Faiths and wholeheartedly encouraged what we today call interreligious dialogue.[9]

According to Teilhard, the central issues which concern all religions today are the understanding of God and transcendence, the value placed on the world and its development (what he calls the "building of the earth"), the importance assigned to the individual person, and the attitudes taken towards humankind and its social needs. Teilhard's affinity lies with the modernizers and progressives of other religions, not with the traditionalists. In the application of evolutionary thinking to religion, he has been compared with Sri Aurobindo, who did the same for Hinduism, and with Mohammed Iqbal, the great reformer of Islam. All three stress the importance of spirituality and mysticism for the world today, the development of spiritual resources needed by individuals and societies.

Long ago Teilhard expressed the hope that our scientific endeavor may be for the good of humanity, that all our efforts, our energies, and money would not longer be lost "in the abyss of armaments and war."[10] Today, more than ever, we need to be reminded of this, that only the forces of love will overcome our divisions, our fear of each other, our politics of hate and persecution, and create the necessary conditions for global peace.

Thus we need a global spirituality. Robert Muller considers the further development of spirituality as the next step necessary in the work of the United Nations in order to bring about the unification of the world rather than its disintegration.

The understanding and practice of spirituality is one of the really big problems for us today. How we face it will determine the future of our world—and whether the world will have a future at all. This plea for spirituality is not a plea for false and evasive "spiritualization." In fact, we must approach the spiritual heritage of Western and Eastern religions in a critical spirit and ask whether spirituality has not been too often divorced from the earth, from society, from the body, from sexuality. Has spirituality not often been the exclusive search for God and the transcendent, for the spirit (with a consequent rejection of matter), particularly by ascetics and monastics? Many spiritualities also include strong antifeminist tendencies, for the spiritual quest has often been the prerogative of men pursuing a spiritual ideal that rejected and excluded women.

To what extent have spiritualities in the past been the prerogative of a social and intellectual elite? To what extent have spiritualities of the past existed in a vacuum of comfort and privilege rather than penetrating and transforming the real problems of life as lived by the multitude of women and men in this world?

When Teilhard de Chardin reflected on the evolution of spirituality, he was in search of a force of integration, a spirituality that could be related to all levels of our experience. Teilhard tried more than most to develop a concretely rooted spirituality, rooted in the experience of the earth and its peoples, rooted in nature, body, and community, rooted in our search for knowledge and the insights of our science. The general principle of his spirituality is the emphasis on *creative transformation*—a spirituality that can transform our work, our thoughts, our prayer, our society, our world, and thus create religious awareness by increasing our sensitivity, our personal integration, and our social responsibility.

When Teilhard spoke of a "new mysticism," he meant a mysticism dynamically oriented towards action; a mysticism which is supremely a mysticism of loving, of the dynamic, all-transforming fire of love which can, if we so believe and wish and work, create the world anew.

Mary and Ellen Lukas introduced their biography of Teilhard[11] with a story from the Auvergne where Teilhard was born. They tell of an Auvergnat legend where the innocent seeker leaves his land, and all he has, to look for the secret at the heart of Reality, the single truth behind the veil of multiple illusion.

In some versions of the story the seeker follows a magic bird of paradise across the world, but he pays a great price for finding this secret: he is wounded in its conquest and forced to walk alone to the end of his life, without being able to communicate what he has found to any other living soul.

Is this story a parable of Teilhard's life the authors ask. When Teilhard died in 1955 in a little apartment in New York, thousands of miles away from the land that first awakened his passion for the scientific and mystical quest, almost unknown and alone, did his vision die with him?

No, for he left us his work as a legacy against oblivion. But it is a work often difficult to understand; it requires considerable effort and still deserves much critical attention and scrutiny. If we make the effort, we can still hear Teilhard's voice and discover a powerful vision which bears witness to a deep faith, a tremendous hope, and most of all, a consuming and compassionate love for the suffering toils of humanity and for the ever-present, ever-living spirit among us. This is a vision which can truly speak to the religious needs of our age, for it offers a spirituality we can live by.

For Teilhard, the human adventure is more than an ascent to knowledge. It is a call to ascend to the height of the spirit, but a spirit who has come down to us and meets us in and through our work-a-day world—if we but learn to see and strive to develop a true mysticism of action which does not lead out of the world, but into it.

## 2

# Socialization and the Future of Humankind

To understand Teilhard de Chardin's thought on the evolution of spirituality, one must take into account his ideas about the further evolution of society, ideas to which he sometimes referred by using the term *socialization*. This term may mean different things to different people, depending on their political leanings or on their ability to understand social processes. While the general reader may easily associate *socialization* with society at large, the professional sociologist uses the term, which gained currency during the 1930s, in the specific sense of denoting "the process by which culture is transmitted from one generation to the next."[1] But this fairly simple definition is not without its ambiguous connotations, and individual sociologists vary considerably in their respective understanding of what this process includes. The socialization of the individual is understood to imply not only the learning of various social roles, but also the transmission of beliefs, values, and other cognitive aspects of a given culture that are transmitted through different socializing agents.

The concept of socialization plays an important role in the writings of Teilhard de Chardin, yet he does not use the term in the narrow sense of specialized sociological discourse. For him it has a predominantly collective meaning; it is a dynamic concept which implies a greater social integration of the whole of humankind than we know at present. The socialization of humankind, understood as a growing collective unity, is not an entirely new phenomenon, but it has become so accelerated today that it seems to possess an altogether new quality. Teilhard interpreted the present signs of socialization as the beginning of a unifying process which needs to be greatly intensified and consciously directed towards a higher aim. Thus socialization becomes in his writings synonymous with terms such as the *planetization* or even the *totalization* of humankind. Understood in this sense, socialization is not simply a given fact, a transmission of culture which can be studied in the past or present; it is a future goal to be brought about, planned, and worked for.

Marx's motto "not to understand the world but to change it" applies today with equal truth, at least as far as the desire for change is concerned, to modern science and technology, and it is also significant in the thought of Teilhard. He was an active scientist who transcended the boundaries of his empirical research by reflecting on the role of science in shaping the future and by discussing the possibilities of a higher future which humankind needs and has to work for.

## 1. Humankind as Organic Collectivity

In *The Phenomenon of Man* Teilhard reflects upon humankind-as-a-whole. He sees the growing unity of human beings as a phenomenon of cosmic and historical extent. In its biological roots the human being is related to the whole development of the cosmos and, even more, to the general phenomenon of life. One may almost call this insertedness into the cosmos our vertical dimension. This vertical line, leading to the distant past, is always supplemented by a horizontal dimension in the present: at each stage of development the human being is inserted into a group. Thus the individual is always related to a larger community although the nature of this relationship may, with the course of time, alter beyond recognition. The social phenomenon is truly universal in the sense that it is present always and everywhere, and that it marks any individual.

However, the nature of the social phenomenon itself—its actual content or practically lived reality—may undergo such qualitative changes that the kind of society people have may completely alter in its organization and complexity.

At present the word *society* is mostly applied to a socially, politically, or racially limited group so that the whole of humankind comprises many different kinds of societies. But it is perfectly possible to imagine, apart from our vertical dimension linked to the past and the horizontal dimension arising from the present, a new vertical pointing to the future where, instead of distinct and separate societies, one single *world society* would emerge. Through the particular conditions of our age, the unification of humankind into a global community is gaining a greater momentum than ever before in history.

It is this dynamic, future-oriented process of unification which Teilhard means when he speaks of socialization. It would require the true integration of all people into a single, though complex and diversified, unity which would ultimately lead to a convergence of humanity at a trans-historical point. Leaving aside the difficult philosophical implications of such ultimate convergence, we shall presently only consider the possibilities and problems of the process of socialization as seen by Teilhard.

The social dimension of the human being has always been recognized by thinkers. However, Teilhard's reflections go beyond the mere recognition of this fact by interpreting the social phenomenon not only through the dynamic categories of development and progress, also found in Marxist philosophy, but by extending the biological dynamic of life to social reality. The "human group" is an organic whole, a biological phylum. The morphological evolution of the human being—the emergence of the present physical form of the individual—is seen to continue in the social evolution of humankind. If evolution has reached its provisional summit in the self-reflective individual, this does not imply that evolution has come to a standstill. Human social evolution must progress further beyond the level reached by contemporary society.

Although social scientists might question the transfer of biological terms to social reality, people coming from the life sciences, for example, Julian Huxley, share Teilhard's conviction about the possibility and, moreover, the necessity of a further evolution of humankind. For Teilhard as for Huxley, the human being is "the ascending arrow of evolution" in whom evolution has grown conscious of itself. Now the further course of evolution depends on human beings themselves. At the present stage of development in knowledge, power, and sheer numbers, a higher socialization of humankind seems to be imperative for human survival. However, a greater social integration of all people will not come about by itself; it demands the strenuous effort of all to build up the earth into a world community.

There are certain signs that strong socializing forces are at work in our contemporary world—numerous attempts to establish healthier, stronger, and more effective social, political, and economic communities. But each of these leaves much to be desired. Teilhard regarded the attempts of different political systems, such as democracy, communism, or fascism, to promote socialization as insufficient, partially because any social integration achieved was reached through external coercion rather than the true union of people. The future needs a new social synthesis in which individuality and collectivity will not exclusively be opposed to each other. In order to reach this synthesis, the forces of socialization would have to be greatly intensified and greater human unity would have to be brought about by free inner choice rather than external coercion.

The achievement of such a synthesis is a formidable task. Its practical realization depends on a crucial question: Is there a future at all for humanity-as-a-whole, that is, is there a goal to be reached, a reason and aim to live for? The problem of the future is paramount for the present: Will humanity survive or be annihilated? Will it progress or stagnate? Various positive and negative answers are possible to these questions, and one's choice depends perhaps mostly on one's basic attitudes and values. Teilhard thought that we have no decisive evidence for either hope or despair regarding the future of humankind, but people today have many more reasons to be pessimistic than was perhaps the case during Teilhard's lifetime. Many contemporary disturbances and difficulties, even the "existential malaise" of certain thinkers, were for him an indication of the general anxiety about the outcome of the future. At the same time he was deeply convinced that despair cannot provide the necessary energy for action; only hope can, and it is essential to stimulate human thought and action so that a higher future for the whole of humankind can be brought about.

## 2. *The Rise of Consciousness*

After having mentioned some of the basic features of the social phenomenon, we may now discuss on what grounds Teilhard expected a *higher* socialization of humankind. If the social phenomenon is taken to be an integral part of evolution, it has to be seen in the total context of our past evolutionary history. Despite the trials and errors of evolution, one can discern a certain general orientation and irreversibility of evolutionary developments. Moreover, several "critical steps" or thresholds can be pointed out in the past, each of which exercised a decisive influence on the further course of evolution. Suffice it here to mention two of the most important critical steps: the advent of life at one given (although not precisely known) moment of time and, much later, the birth of thought within life. The "rise of consciousness" in the universe was a collective event before the development and progress of individual self-reflection could take place. As the history of the entire cosmos is important for the right understanding of the human being, so, in turn, the emergence of thought is decisive for seeing the course of evolution in its proper perspective. Consciousness is neither a simple by-product of evolution nor a fortuitous anomaly, nor is it merely a superstructure of matter; it is the very key to understanding evolution itself, the central evolutionary phenomenon. After the birth of consciousness in the universe, any further progress of evolution must be measured by the progress of thought. The "natural evolution" is linked up with and continued by a "cultural evolution." Teilhard refers to this further evolution as the expansion and growth of the "noosphere," the growing layer of thought encircling the earth above and beyond the layer of mere life.

Up to now, we have been wont to regard the achievements

of the individual thinker, artist, or genius as the ultimate height human thought can attain. Yet although human history may, to a large extent, have been shaped by great personalities, even the most personal achievement has never been an entirely individual accomplishment, isolated from the context of a given society. Today, however, we can observe more than this traditional relationship between the individual and society; we notice a further rise in consciousness through the steady increase in human interthinking. A new kind of coreflection is emerging. If this trend continues, and we have many reasons to believe it will, it will lead to a greater concentration and intensity of thought than ever known before.

### 3. One World Civilization

People may wonder why we should expect a collective consciousness at this moment in history when in the past consciousness has always been the noblest prerogative of the individual. Why should we wait and work for one world civilization beyond the series of civilizations with which human history is studded throughout? When we study the gradual unfolding of different cultures, the inevitable question arises: Are all these civilizations in their overwhelming diversity only variations on the same theme, endlessly repeated, of rise and fall? Is there no fundamental advance *beyond* this level of repetitive successions? Teilhard was fond of reminding those who may quote the wisdom of the ages and the accumulated experience of the wide span of human history, how infinitely longer the cosmos has endured. In comparison with the vast geological timescale, the period of human history is dwarflike. It is by no means a warranted conclusion, therefore, that the past is an adequate guide to the present or the future.

Today, the human species has covered the entire globe so that there is little room left for expansion. The inevitably greater physical contact between people, exponentially increased by the modern network of communications, is leading to a true "globalization" of the human phenomenon. The sheer numbers of humanity with their increasing interdependence and the constant pressures on the total resources of the earth produce a "compression" or "infolding" of humanity upon itself. The possibility for further geographical expansion, given all through historical time up to very recently, has come to an end and there is, at present at least, little prospect for an escape outside this globe of ours. The "human tide" is rising, an almost irresistible movement of the mass of all human beings towards a collective awareness of their intrinsic belonging together.

The enormous development of science and technology and the explosion of knowledge greatly accelerate this process of unification. The increasingly important role of consciously guided research and planning can be observed everywhere. These pursuits can no longer be the exclusive task of isolated individuals, but involve an ever larger number of people. If to think meant in the past to withdraw and isolate oneself, it now means more and more thinking together in a group. Thus human reflection itself is becoming "socialized" by gradually developing into coreflection. Illuminating contemporary examples of growing coreflection are provided by the processes of consciousness-raising active among many groups of the poor and oppressed in search of liberation, not least among women.

It is also interesting to note that the traditional idea of the lonely scholar working in a study has largely become obsolete as most research is now done in teamwork. Nor may science be regarded as a fortuitous activity as it has become a vital necessity for humankind. If science was originally born "of the exuberance of an internal activity that had outstripped the material needs of life; . . . of the curiosity of dreamers and idlers," it is now no longer "an accessory occupation . . . but an essential activity, a natural derivative of the overspill of energy constantly liberated by mechanization. We can envisage a world whose constantly increasing "leisure" and heightened interest would find their vital issue in fathoming everything, trying everything, extending everything . . ."[2]

One single world civilization may gradually evolve. It is essential, however, to ask whether this oneness would merely mean an external coming together of all human beings or whether it would bring with it a better kind of society. Does the idea of the future of humankind simply imply survival, that is, the continuation of human existence as we now know it, or could the future hold a kind of "superlife"[3] in store, that is, a qualitative improvement of present life? According to Teilhard, it is people's ambition today not only to survive or live well, but to live better and to be more, to "superlive" by reaching out into some higher domain of consciousness and action.

Thus the envisaged "superlife" of humankind implies more than only a complexification of society. When Teilhard speaks of socialization, one might be easily misled into thinking that he was exclusively concerned with more and more complex processes irrespective of the individual. Although the complexification of society is much stressed, it must not be understood to mean a more complicated and disordered society. On the contrary, it stands for a better organization and arrangement of human society, that is, ultimately for the establishment of more order.[4] In a postscript to *The Phenomenon of Man*, written ten years after its completion, Teilhard described the social phase of human evolution as "the ascent towards a collective threshold of reflection," a second stage of hominization whose final success is by no means inevitable or certain, although this process of collective reflection is characterized by certain irreversible features. One of these is a "revealing association of technical organisation and inward spiritual concentration."[5]

Personalization and socialization are not opposed; they are complementary. Consequently, the Teilhardian sense of socialization must not be confused with a totalitarian organization of human society or with the submergence of the individual in the total mass of humanity. The higher society which he envisages centers around the confluence of human thought. The latter is a collective reality *sui generis*, a new whole, whose value transcends the sum total of its constituent parts. This new reality is ultimately "only definable as a mind."[6]

Personalization can be so closely related to socialization because it stands for something quite different from individuality. To be a person implies an internal deepening, concentration, and intensification of consciousness, while individuality is merely external separateness from others. The person is supremely centered but at the same time radiates outwards: people reach out towards others and can truly find themselves only in and through union with others. Thus a higher socialization, understood in its right sense, might mean the beginning of the era of person rather than its end. Ultimately, it is the quality of our human relationships that matters most. This problem is coming more and more to the fore today as people are beginning to realize that we may have dealt competently with machines without having come to terms with our relationships with others or ourselves. Educationists, too, are stressing that the quality of relationships rather than the educational technique employed is decisive in the education of human beings towards maturity and growth.

### 4. The Future as Human Task

The education and general orientation of people toward the future is vital for the course and eventual outcome of the future. Humanity now bears full responsibility for its own future. This is an immense challenge which can only be met if we thoroughly prepare ourselves for this task. The kind of future we will get will depend to a large extent on the quality of people who shape it. Teilhard emphasized the need for a *homo progressivus*,[7] a progressive, future-oriented and future-affirming being with wide, open awareness—a person who has the energy of thought to recognize the problems of the future and find their solutions, and the energy of action to put them into practice.

One of the greatest problems at present is: Can we utilize the resources at our disposal in such a way that we can plan and effectively bring about a better future for a more united humankind? The solution to this problem would include, among other things, the prevention of war, the establishment and preservation of peace, the qualitative improvement of interracial and international relationships, and perhaps also the eventual foundation of a world government. The realization of these goals, whose success is at present by no means guaranteed, depends ultimately on the quality of human thought and action. The latter, however, are not only dependent on the available scientific means, but are intrinsically related to the philosophical, spiritual, moral, and religious resources of the entire world community.

Teilhard de Chardin was a great pioneer in calling attention to the problem of the future. From the late thirties onwards he often spoke and wrote about this topic; he turned his thought to it immediately at the end of the Second World War and later, in the fifties, he insisted again and again on the need for a scientific study of the future. Today, there is a greater general awareness of this problem, as can be seen from the new science of "futurology" and many publications dealing with vital policy issues affecting the future of humankind.

Modern thinkers such as the American architect Buckminster Fuller or the German nuclear physicist-philosopher C.F. von Weizsäcker have been much concerned with the future. Professor Fuller has stressed again and again that we must realize that "our spaceship Earth" is in fact "a closed system." Assessing this situation he has said, "Quite clearly our task is predominantly metaphysical—for it is how to get all of humanity to educate itself swiftly enough to generate spontaneous social behaviors which will avoid extinction."

Pleading for a holistic approach to human progress, he has warned against our society's persistent increase of educational and employment specialization when it is scientifically well documented "that biological extinction is always occasioned by over-specialization. Specialization's preoccupation with parts deliberately forfeits the opportunity to apprehend and comprehend,"[8] which can only be given by viewing a whole beyond its separate parts. If the present trend towards greater specialization continues, it might well prove lethal and lead to the extinction of our species.

Long ago, Professor C.F. von Weizsäcker, in a lecture on "The Conditions of World Peace" given at the India International Centre, New Delhi (1969), emphasized that an extraordinary ethical and moral effort is needed to ensure not only humanity's future survival but, even more, its progress. He also argued that the transformation of our entire political and social system is an absolute prerequisite for the future. These ideas show a great affinity with Teilhard's approach to the problem of the future.

The past-present-oriented "learning of social roles" is no longer sufficient; we need a future-oriented process of socialization both at the individual and collective level. The social integration of all people into a kind of "super-humanity" presupposes the scientifically investigated and consciously planned further self-evolution of human beings towards a higher order. Like most of his contemporaries, Teilhard takes it for granted that a basic mutation has already taken place in modern post-Darwinian, post-Marxian, and post-Freudian consciousness, but he postulates yet another necessary mutation: a greater awareness of humanity's necessary collectivity and the emergence of a higher collective consciousness, composed of innumerable individuals, just as the individual brain is formed of innumerable cells. It appears that for Teilhard, reaching a higher collective organization and consciousness is not only a necessary goal, but also, perhaps, an inevitable one. The higher socialization of humanity or its collectivization is for him part of the great sweeping movement of evolution; he even refers to it as an "irresistible physical process."[9]

This emphasis on an almost irresistible and inevitable movement of socialization makes Teilhard's view differ from that of other thinkers. It has been said that his predominantly biological perspective of evolution does not leave sufficient room for the specifically human and presents too naturalistic a view of human history.[10] Thus Teilhard has been criticized for his failure to recognize "the specific nature of the level of the social" and for equating social progress simply with one of the aspects of biological progress while it is, in fact, much more.[11] Against this view it could be argued that although Teilhard understood human evolution very much from an overall biological perspective, his new understanding of the human being enabled him to approach biology and the entire dynamic of evolution from a new angle. He tried to work out an integrated dialectic of both biological and social life in the form of a progressively evolving pattern of emergence, divergence into different forms, and final convergence at all levels of life. Thus he arrived at a unifying vision of humankind-as-a-whole-in-cosmos-and-history. It may also be said that his firm personal belief in a finally successful outcome of evolution was primarily due to his deep Christian faith.[12] It was in the light of this faith that he interpreted the data of evolution available to him.

## 5. *The Need for and the Ambiguity of Research*

Teilhard's deep belief in the final success of evolution did not prevent him from stressing again and again the enormous importance of the contribution of human beings in bringing about a higher form of socialization. For achieving this aim, he considered the use of research in all areas of human activity to be absolutely vital and necessary. The steadily increasing growth of research and its important role for any planning are already a sign of people's coming together; furthermore, they are a necessary means for creating a common awareness. Teilhard looked at research as such a noble and humanizing effort that, at times, he even considered it a form of adoration.

Research has come to an important turning point: it is no longer only the nature-given resources and energies that are investigated and utilized (as earlier scientists did almost fortuitously). We have developed a qualitatively different kind of research where the very springs of nature are manipulated at far too great a cost, as we know from our current ecological crisis.

The qualitative change in research is evident in the physicist working on the nuclear structure of the atom, the geneticist decoding the genetic structure, and the psychoanalyst analyzing and manipulating the human psyche. The advance of these and other sciences has been so rapid since Teilhard's death in 1955 that the question about the general direction of research has become as urgent as it is alarming. Among the highly exciting— and problematic—research experiments affecting the future of humankind and raising vast new ethical issues are the experiments in the manipulation of the genetic code and thus in human inheritance, the transplantation of human organs and the growth of replacement organs from cells, and human fertilization outside the womb. Given these new developments, an urgent question is becoming ever more urgent: What do we want the human being to be?

Apart from the potential biochemical and psychoanalytical manipulation of the individual, there is the enormous scientific and human problem of world population control. It has been said that the three major tasks which have to be solved during the last part of the twentieth century are population control, security, and development. Teilhard was convinced that the population explosion presents us with entirely new needs and difficulties. Thinking of the future on a global scale, he said, "The problem of building a healthy Mankind . . . is growing more acute every day."[13] He often referred to the need for eugenics, understood in the sense of building a healthy population. Health would embrace every aspect of human development, not merely the physical. Population control is not an exclusively quantitative problem whose solution can simply be found in the reduction or stabilization of human numbers. Teilhard always stressed the need for a qualitative improvement in a given population, and the scientific possibility of a more effective "quality control" may well be given in the future. The ensuing interference with procreative and hereditary processes requires much thought and raises difficult ethical issues, as is evident from much contemporary debate on current developments in biology and medicine.

### 6. Education towards the Future

The appeal to sustain and improve human resources refers to all resources: physical, mental, and spiritual. It is not only change at the biological and psychological level that will alter us but education, too, will have an important role to play in reorienting and preparing us for a new age. Teilhard especially stressed the need to feed the fundamental psychological drive in humans to *want* to evolve. A higher socialization of humankind can only be brought about if people have the will and energy to work for it, if they deeply believe in the positive value of the future. Therefore, people need to be educated towards such a future-affirming and animating belief; they need to be educated towards human oneness and the creation of a global community. At present, our greatest enemies are human isolation, indifference, despair, and pessimism because they destroy "the taste for life."

We have to preserve, animate, and increase our zest for life; otherwise the future, that is a higher future for all, will be impossible.

Teilhard proposed that the science of anthropology should become a truly comprehensive study of the human phenomenon in the past, present, and future. This study would include a generalized "energetics" concerned with "the maintenance and development in man of evolutionary 'drive'. . .the 'activation' of human energy."[14] This could also serve as a motto for all educational efforts of the future. In order to feed the zest for life, the spiritual resources of humankind are as necessary as the physical ones—perhaps even more so. Teilhard emphasized the need for people in general (not merely the engineers who are organizing the material resources of the earth) to define and propagate the aims of human effort and to give humanity a goal and vision to live by. One of the highest aims is the animation of the forces of love, without whose energies a higher socialization of humankind is impossible.

Though mainly tentative and exploratory, Teilhard's ideas on socialization and the future of humankind are nevertheless highly suggestive. They cannot be taken as matter-of-fact statements about what the future *will* be, but they present an inspiring vision of what it *might* be if people committed themselves to a common good beyond the purely material. In a period of turmoil and difficulties, these ideas provide a model for action which could guide human aspirations towards an ultimate union of love. Teilhard's synthesis is already exercising a strong influence on many thinkers and ordinary people in the world who are aware of the urgent need to feed the faith in life. We have to love life in order to live it fully; we have to aspire always higher and beyond in order to create a better future. If a greater social integration and coherence of humankind may seem rather utopian to some, let them be reminded of C.F. von Weizsäcker's statement that human imagination in the past was never great enough to imagine the kind of future that actually became the present.

To appreciate more fully Teilhard's ideas on the future of

## 3

# The One and the Many

RELIGIOUS PERSPECTIVES ON THE INDIVIDUAL AND COMMUNITY IN
CONTEMPORARY CULTURE

We live in an age where many have lost hope. Instead of
social progress, justice, and peace, we experience dissension and
warfare and suffer from the inflexibility of outdated institutions.
We are faced with what appears to be an ever more complex
and anonymous society where the individual experiences
loneliness, alienation, and the impersonality of large organizations
so characteristic of modern life.

One can examine the social, scientific, political, educational,
and other reasons for this state of affairs, yet one may also reflect
on the spiritual dimensions of this contemporary tension between
the individual and society and ask what a religious perspective
may contribute to our understanding.

If the individual and society are in a crisis today and this
crisis can ultimately be understood as a spiritual crisis—that is
to say, a crisis of consciousness—can the great world religions
contribute something to the recovery of the individual? Can they
help to overcome individualistic loneliness and point to the forms
of true community? Can a religious and philosophical reflection

help us in understanding our true self in relationship to others?

Some may think no new lifestyle will evolve from the old religions. It is quite true that religions do not possess any ready recipes for the cure of all our ills. Yet they can offer beliefs, values, and reflections on the inner life which may animate our thought, influence our actions, and transform our being. The teachings of the great religions belong to the global heritage of humankind. In a study of the individual and society, they ought to be critically examined as perhaps our most precious inheritance.

At the present stage of human development a greater unity seems imperative for survival. The necessary integration of humankind and the shaping of a global society require a new social synthesis in which individuality and collectivity will not be exclusively opposed. We need new creative thinking to achieve this synthesis, but it will not come about without inner and outer transformation. Whether religious traditions will be sufficiently creative to inspire such new thinking may, in fact, prove to be the acid test of their vitality as religions, their test of being a living force in the lives of people.

We want to look at the individual and community from a religious perspective in the widest sense of the word; *religious*, not in the sense of any particular denomination or faith, but in the sense of important spiritual values, central for a *Weltanschauung* of today.

Different religions have looked at the relationship of the one and the many, of the individual and society, in a variety of ways. We shall proceed in three stages: First of all, we shall consider the teachings of Eastern and Western religions on the individual and community. Secondly, as the relationship of the one and the many was one of the central concerns of Teilhard de Chardin, we shall discuss his views on the relationship between the individual and community. Thirdly, we shall relate our findings to the situation of the individual and community in contemporary culture. We shall discuss how far religious teachings may help to resolve existing conflicts and provide creative energy for people's lives in cooperation with others.

## 1. *Eastern and Western Religious Teaching on the Individual and Community*

If we compare some of the major belief systems in the history of humankind, we soon realize that the problem of the one and the many, of the individual and society, has been dealt with in a variety of ways. Civilizations tend to emphasize the importance of either the individual or society. The great exception seems to be in Chinese thought, in which the one cannot be without the many, nor can the many be without the one. The solution to the apparent conflict between the one and the many lies, for the Chinese, in the answer that each involves and penetrates the other. This is a very balanced and harmonious view, perhaps also the least specifically "religious," if we think of "religious" as something personal, apart from the social, as something concerned with the supramundane rather than with the here and now.

Looking at specifically religious teaching, we would expect that religions, by definition, must be community-oriented. The adherence of an individual to a particular religion is not an individualistic, private affair in the sense that only one individual partakes in this religion. On the contrary, one shares beliefs and religious practices with others; one joins a community of believers, in whatever form. Thus, one's very adherence to a particular religion acknowledges and establishes the importance of the community, even if the religious teaching may ultimately inspire one's withdrawal from society at large.

Many religious communities have in fact been, or still are, small communities apart from and outside the larger society—a community of the chosen few, the small elite, the sect. However, we are not concerned here with analyzing the different types of religious groups which may exist in particular societies. We rather wish to look at some of the great religious traditions which have shaped entire civilizations and cultures. What do the religions in the East and the West have to say about the individual and community? What is the true nature of the individual, what is the real self? How do self and society relate to each other?

Let us begin with Indian religious thought, whose major focus centers around the realization of the true self. The individual in his or her empirical existence, in the here and now, is bound by ignorance and suffering, especially by ignorance about the true nature of the self. However, suffering implicitly bears within it the germ of spirituality. Freedom from bondage is possible through self-control and self-realization. Spiritual discipline has as its goal the progressive realization of the pure self as distinct from the body. The essence of self-control is to bring about a change in oneself and not in one's environment. Thus the wisdom acquired does not transform the world, but only the individual's attitude towards it. In Indian terms, control over nature without control over oneself, that is to say, self-restraint, can only lead to rivalry, domination, and conflict. The basic problem remains a spiritual one. Spiritual life ranks higher than rational life. The avowed aim of the human being is spiritual realization: freedom from bondage for the Hindu, the attainment of Nirvana for the Buddhist.

This strong emphasis on spiritual realization in Indian religions has led to the development of an intensive spiritual individualism. The relationship to the Absolute or to God became more important than people's relationships to each other. In fact, the individual was taught how to be indifferent to the many relationships. The social nature of the human being did not receive the same attention in Indian thought as the relationship to God, which is perhaps worked out in greater detail, with more depth and richness, than in other religions. Similarly, the spiritual nature of the human being, the soul, has received more emphasis in Indian religion than elsewhere. The particular contribution of Indian religious thought to our global religious heritage may, in fact, lie in these two areas. But because of these emphases, it has also often been pointed out that the dominant trend of Indian religions is one of idealism and monism, of "other-worldliness" to the neglect of "this-worldliness." In practice this may not always be true and reality may be much more complex. Whatever the case may be, the social nature of the human being did not receive the attention it deserved in India. Social virtues are only necessary for so long as people live in society. However, a distinctive feature of the Indian religious ideal is that one should rise above society, be liberated from it by living a life of renunciation. This is, of course, never totally attainable, to live completely outside society. Sometimes this was realized and acknowledged as, for example, in the teachings of the Bhagavad-Gita. By and large, however, the Indian ideal of renunciation, as traditionally understood and practiced, was an antisocial ideal.

We have the paradoxical situation that Indian religions teach a highly individualistic religious ideal which sets the individual apart from and outside society while, in actual social practice, during membership in society, the individual is governed by a rigid social structure which traditionally allows for little development of individuality. The main concepts which governed the place of the individual in traditional Indian society were those of duties and obligations towards others, individuals, or the gods. The traditional social structure of Hinduism, particularly in the complex form of the caste system as both a religious and social phenomenon, included many anti-individual practices.

In traditional India, secular, social or political thought relating to the rights of the individual or the nature of society did not develop to the same extent as in the West. Only relatively recently in Indian history has the idea of a whole Indian community and of a nationhood of the Indian people developed. Secular and humanitarian thought, introduced into India from the outside, became concerned with the role of the individual and the whole community. In a great man like Mahatma Gandhi, we can see how traditional religious teaching was creatively transformed to produce a new and original approach to the relationship between the individual and society.

If we now consider Chinese thought on the individual and society, we almost seem to reach the antithesis of Indian thought. The expressed aim, particularly of Confucian teaching, is to achieve a harmonious balance between the individual and society. From birth to death one does not exist in isolation but in and through social relationships. One lives as an individual, but one does so only in society. Within the framework of society, the individual should be able to realize his or her human nature to the fullest extent. By doing this, one will also be able to develop the nature of others to the fullest. Thus, the cultivation of the individual character is the root of all social well-being and harmony.

This cultivation of the individual includes both inward steps of perfection and outward steps, relating to others, to family and society. We thus have a qualitative interrelationship between the individual and society. Society is not simply an aggregate of so many individuals; it is a dynamic and organic unity permanently shaped by the quality of the character of its individuals. Consequently, a society can only be as good as its members. What ultimately matters most is the quality of human relationships. An outstanding characteristic of Chinese social thought is the emphasis on obligations rather than the rights of the individual in relationship to society—a theme which we are just getting around to thinking about in the West.

For the Chinese, the way to self-realization is more empirically conceived than in the more idealistically-oriented Indian thought. Confucius said, "If we are not yet able to serve man, how can we serve spiritual beings?" The search for a harmonious balance between the individual and the community does not allow for an exclusively "religious" or "spiritual" quest as an escape or flight from other people, from society, from the world at large. The great and admirable genius of classical Chinese thought lies in this perfectly harmonious blend between the one and the many, the synthesis between the universal and the particular, so strong a Chinese trait that it even affected a transformation of Buddhism when it arrived from India.

In comparison to Indian and Chinese religions, Islam and Judaism are often seen to stress primarily the community over and above the individual. Islamic teaching emphasizes the cooperative and collective functioning of human beings in society, but it also teaches an essential equality of all human beings. From its beginning, Islam was concerned with the establishment of a social order and the conduct of social practice. However, responsibility for action before God lies ultimately with the individual. From early on in the history of Islam, there existed a strong tension between the established religion of Islamic society, the social religion, and the personal "religion of the heart" taught by the Sufi orders. This permanent tension sometimes threatened the very fabric of Islamic society, for many medieval Sufi movements tended to an exclusive individualism in their pursuit of a religious ideal. Great Islamic teachers were able to exercise restraint and restore a certain balance between the orthodoxy of Islamic society and the mystical quest of individual Sufis. The introduction of modern science and technology has, in turn, brought with it new and complex problems for the idea of an Islamic society with which we cannot deal here.

If we look at the relationship between the individual and society in the Judaeo-Christian tradition, we see that for the ancient Hebrews, the religious and national community originally took precedence over the individual in Israel's early history. But later on, individuals emerged slowly in their own right. The Hebrew prophets addressed themselves to both individual and community and expressed the individual's reponsibility to God and fellow men in the strongest terms. The most important teaching for the understanding of the position of the individual is the biblical doctrine that the human being is created in the image of God. This doctrine of creation implies that, in being called from nothing, the individual is dependent on God for continued existence. At the same time, the individual carries full responsibility for his or her actions. Being an individual as such is never the source of evil, although the individual can radically misuse the gift of freedom.

The New Testament contains many sayings addressed to the individual but also many parables where the community is central. All later Christian thought presents this tension between the individual in direct relationship to God, and the individual as being related to God only insofar as he or she participates in the life of others and is incorporated into a community. St. Paul insists especially on the integral unity of the individual; each person is a living unity of mind, body, and spirit. The individual cannot be exclusively identified with simply one of these aspects, nor can individuals be reduced to one of their functions in society. Paul also emphasizes the interdependence of individual and community—exemplified for him in the community of the church—by stressing that each person shall bear his burden while it is incumbent on all members of the community to bear one another's burdens.

Three important points that persistently occur in Christian

teaching about the individual and community are:

a. The individual person is acknowledged as a fundamental type of being created by God, and each individual is unique. Individuality remains an ultimate trait.

b. The individual person is addressed by God as a responsible being who possesses a finite or conditioned freedom.

c. The individual person is essentially involved with other individuals in view of the fact that the divine life is envisaged as a community of persons whose symbol of ultimate perfection is the divine kingdom.

Several of these ideas are so much part of the Western cultural tradition that they have become integrated into our secular thinking about the individual, while Christian thought about the community has perhaps not been developed to quite the same extent. Christian theologians have speculated about the nature of the kingdom of God in the past, yet frequently these speculations have little direct relevance for the enormous tasks facing our societies today.

Can we retain anything from the religious teachings about the individual and community? Yes and no. Our very brief investigation suggests that the great religions tend to emphasize either the individual or the community; a harmonious balance is only rarely achieved. If we could combine some of the harmony between the human being and society, as taught by the Chinese, with some of the deep insights about the human person in some other religions, this could be very beneficial for the moral and spiritual education of our contemporaries. At the same time we must be aware that many of our difficulties are so new and complex that they cannot be satisfactorily solved by ancient teachings which emanated from homogenous societies living in geographically limited areas. It is in a dynamic and creative way that we must reflect on these religious teachings about the nature of the human being, the individual's place in society, and the importance of a well-organized community. Only then may we find the necessary inspiration and guidance to create a new synthesis which will meet our contemporary needs in an adequate way.

For most people the word *society* still applies only to a socially, politically, or racially limited group. In this sense, humankind consists of many different societies. But must we not think much more in terms of the emergence of one world society? On a global scale the relationship of individual and society assumes quite different proportions. We do not possess any adequate model for this complexity in any religious teaching of the past. Religions have emerged and were founded as small communities. Yet religious teachers have addressed themselves primarily to the individual and preached a "change of heart." All the major religions have provided individual models of perfection, holiness, and mysticism—but is this enough for a new society? How can we relate this individualistically-oriented spirituality to our great numbers, to the problems of social action, to social progress, justice, and peace?

In trying to answer this question, we may find inspiration in the thought of Pierre Teilhard de Chardin, who, thirty, forty, even fifty years ago, reflected on the one and the many, the relationship of the individual to the group, and of the group to the individual.

## 2. Teilhard de Chardin's Thought on the Individual and Community

In one of Teilhard's major works, *The Phenomenon of Man*, he sees man, both the species and the individual, as being vertically inserted into the history of the cosmos, and horizontally inserted into the group. The social phenomenon is truly universal in that it is present always and everywhere; it marks the development of each individual. Each of us is always related to a larger community, although the nature of this relationship may, during the course of time, alter beyond recognition. Thus the nature of the social phenomenon itself is undergoing qualitative changes at the moment because the organization and complexity of society are changing. The social phenomenon is steadily growing, like a spiral drawing more and more closely together towards a summit where a true world community beyond the mere agglomeration of individuals might be realized. Through the conditions of our age, the unification of humankind is gaining momentum. At the same time, it seems to be more torn apart than ever, faced with the threat of being fragmented into opposed and warring units. At the present stage of human development in knowledge, power, and sheer numbers, a higher social integration of humankind seems to be imperative and is a task of ever greater urgency for human survival.

Teilhard refers to this task as the "socialization" or sometimes the "planetization" or even "totalization" of humankind—ugly words with a predominantly collective meaning. They imply a greater social integration, the emergence of a global society beyond what we know at present. This socialization is a new phenomenon in history, an urgent task in the future evolution of humankind. But it will not come about by itself; it is a goal which has to be planned and worked for, requiring the strenuous effort of all human beings. Thus Teilhard understands the complexity of modern society, of which we see ever more signs, only as the beginning of a unifying process which needs to be greatly intensified and consciously directed towards a higher aim. For him, humankind shares not only common roots, a common origin, but also a common destiny.

There is no going back in the development of consciousness, even though there may be individual setbacks. Similarly, there is no going back to earlier and simpler forms of society, only a going forward to a higher complexity, a qualitatively better integration. People may be frightened by this vision and misunderstand it as a totalitarian utopia; they may experience it as a threat to their individuality which they fear to lose. But Teilhard, not unlike the ancient Chinese, saw society and the individual as inextricably interrelated; the value of one enhances the value and development of the other. There are certain socializing forces at work in our contemporary world, numerous attempts to establish stronger and more effective social, political, and economic communities. Yet Teilhard regarded the attempts of existing political systems, whether they be democracy, socialism, communism, or fascism, to promote a better society as insufficient. Whatever social integration they may have achieved has largely been through external coercion. Their attempts do not yet represent the true union of people through the forces of love and attraction.

Teilhard very much envisaged the emergence of one civilization, of what others have called the "civilization of the universal." Today, human reflection itself is becoming socialized by gradually developing into some forms of interthinking, some kind of coreflection. Teilhard was concerned not only with humanity's survival, understood as the continuation of human existence as we now know it; he inquired also into the possibility of a qualitatively different kind of life in a different society with different individuals. He was interested not merely in surviving or in living well, but in living better—not in the materialistic sense of having more, consuming more, acquiring more wealth and affluence. On the contrary, to live better means to develop a higher, more enriched personal consciousness, to pursue more satisfactory work, to promote greater social harmony. This qualitative difference would imply a high degree of freedom and choice for the individual. The greatest deficiency of the socializing forces at present is their use of force and coercion. Love alone can lead to the deepest affinity and integration among people. Teilhard reckoned with love as a form of energy as important in the universe as the energy of matter. The energy of love unifies and builds up; it integrates and synthesizes different elements into a higher unity—it creates unanimization, as Teilhard says.

Thus a higher socialization of humankind does not simply mean a greater external complexity of society, a better arrangement and organization of its members; it also implies a greater order and a qualitative difference in the way of life.

Through higher socialization, the individual person, far from being oppressed, should find greater personal awareness and realization of himself or herself. For Teilhard, personalization and socialization are interdependent and complementary rather than opposed to each other. A more complex organization of human society must not be confused with the notion of a totalitarian political system or with the submergence or oppression of the individual by society. For Teilhard, personalization – that is to say, becoming a person – is something quite different from merely being an individual. To be a person implies the internal deepening and intensification of consciousness, both its inner concentration and its expansion, while individuality merely means external separateness from others. The person is supremely centered but radiates out at the same time. The person reaches out towards others and can truly find himself or herself only in and through union with others. Teilhard thus understands personalization as a process of growth and progressive centration: the centering of oneself first, then the centering upon another person, and lastly, the centering together upon something greater and higher. He has expressed this in his *Reflections on Happiness*:

> True happiness is a happiness of growth . . . characterized by: 1. unification of self within our own selves; 2. union of our own being with other beings who are our equals; 3. subordination of our own life to a life which is greater than ours.[1]

When Teilhard speaks about the one and the many, he means the relationship between the individual and the community of humanity, not just one particular society. To relate to all of humanity and seek its greater harmony, the individual needs to cultivate a universal form of love, a love which transcends the unifying forces of sexual love, of friendship and of patriotism, the love of one's country. To unite the multiplicity which is humankind in such a way as not only to safeguard but, indeed, to enhance and perfect the person – that was Teilhard's idea of socialization. He envisaged a new social synthesis where individuality and collectivity were not opposed to each other. But he was by no means certain that people would achieve such a synthesis. Without a creative effort on the part of all it will be impossible.

Teilhard saw the contemporary crisis, both in its individual and social dimensions, very much as a spiritual crisis: the individual and the world in search of a soul. He perceived a crisis of reflection and consciousness which expresses itself as a crisis in interpersonal relationships and a crisis in the meaning of life and the universe. Both person and society have become problematic; the whole movement of life and all human achievement may be threatened by a retrogressive movement of individualism.

To be grouped together by merely external forces will tend to depersonalize us. Unless the growing complexity of society is inspired by love and thus placed at the service of personalization, it will become merely destructive. In *The Phenomenon of Man* Teilhard wrote: "We are distressed and pained when we see modern attempts at human collectivisation ending up, contrary to our expectations...in a lowering and enslavement of consciousness."[2]

Because we have neglected the forces of personalization, we have arrived at mechanization. What Teilhard wanted was not to go backward and give the individual more external room, but to go "beyond the collective" by increasing the complexity, the higher and better order of society, while at the same time enhancing the inner self-awareness of the individual. Teilhard was well aware that one cannot love a collectivity as such; one needs a face and a heart to love, a presence, he used to say, and for him this presence was found in the presence of God at all stages of human history and in all phases of human encounter.

One human society, more fully and positively integrated than we may be able to conceive at present, will only come about if people so wish and work for it. Humankind needs to want to evolve, needs to believe in the positive value of the future in order to be able to strive for it. Thus individuals require to be educated towards such future-affirming belief; they need to be educated towards human oneness, towards a community beyond the individual rather than merely reaffirming the place of the individual in society.

Tremendous external threats are endangering the very fabric of human society, threats created and controlled by individuals and, even more, by groups. Psychologically speaking, our greatest enemies are human isolation, indifference, and despair because they destroy "man's taste for life," for the right kind of life, a better quality of life and a higher aim in life.

Teilhard was particularly concerned with the activation of human energy towards such a higher aim, understood as the furtherance of greater social unity linked to deeper personal dignity. One of the urgent requirements of contemporary society is the need for people to be able to define and propagate the aims of human effort. One of the highest aims would be the animation of the forces of love. We are so wont to assess the material energy resources available to our society and to humankind as a whole, but do we ever think of the spiritual energy resources available to us today? Where do we find our love and zest for life? How can we increase and strengthen them? How can we increase our ability to love and care?

Teilhard saw the great religions as the deepest sources of spiritual energy. This does not mean that we have to return to an earlier so-called golden age of religious beliefs and practices, not does it mean that religions possess, or ever did possess, the answers to all our problems. It is only through a dynamic spirituality oriented towards the present and the future that we can become animated and strengthened. Teilhard saw religion as a life-enhancing and not a life-negating force. The phenomenon of religion is an integral part of the human phenomenon. The very center and core of the phenomenon of religion is a rightly understood spirituality and mysticism, a spiritual vision of oneness between God, the world, and all people which, at the same time, is full of rich and stark concreteness. This was Teilhard's ultimate understanding of the one and the many and it was in this perspective that he could see both spirit and matter united and transformed, and the individual and the community find their mutual harmony and fulfillment.

This is an inspiring vision; it may animate and sustain the life of many individuals today, but it is not reality as we know it. What conclusions can we draw, then, from these ideas for ourselves today, for the situation of the individual and the community in contemporary culture?

## 3. *The Individual and Community in Contemporary Culture*

Many today speak about the plight of the individual and a widespread sense of alienation. But is there not also a sense in which the individual has gained greater autonomy and strength, freedom from fears and constraints quite unknown in the past? Erich Fromm pointed out in his book *The Fear of Freedom* (1960) that the emergence of the individual or the process of individuation is always two-sided, consisting of both growing self-strength and growing aloneness. The history of the human species also follows such a process of individuation and growing freedom. But there are limits to this growth, partly set by individual and partly by social consideration. Our problem is how this growth of self and society can be furthered in an interdependent and cooperative manner rather than in a competitive way. At present, the alienation of the individual from himself and others seems to be partly due to the one-sided emphasis on impersonal, objective knowledge and the preponderant stress on rationalism in Western culture, both of which have brought about a crisis in self-knowledge. Furthermore, the development of the technological society has brought with it the idea of the human being as an interchangeable part in an impersonal system where the uniqueness of human life and of the person is sacrificed. We have also witnessed an unprecedented growth of totalitarian governments which deprive the individual of rights and individuality. However, the solution of the tension or conflict between the individual and society does not lie in a unilateral affirmation of the rights of the individual as against the state, as we are made to believe in some political speeches. A much more fruitful approach is represented by pursuing the cooperation of individual and society for their mutual, interdependent development.

Let us first look at the individual, and then at society. What is relevant for the development of the individual? Many would put education first, but are our educational goals not wrongly oriented and in need of reexamination? Adam Curle, in his book *Education for Liberation*[3] pleads for a radical reconsideration of our priorities. He thinks that "improvement in the future will mean the increasing perfection of man's nature,"[4] an aim to which technology has little contribution to make, although it may remove adverse conditions.

We need to work on the central core of the human being rather than only on problems of the environment, outer space, or material and scientific advance. What we need is an increase in the average level of awareness, an awareness which comes from an examined life in the Socratic sense. Curle thinks that most people seem to have a greater belonging-identity than real awareness. The identity of their self is rooted in what belongs to them, whether these belongings are material things, education, or people; and what they belong to, a family, profession, religion, society, etc. But the core of a person lies in the total sense of self behind the often distracting activities of mind and emotion. To the extent that we are self-aware, we are liberated from obsessive self-concern; we are more able to turn to other people and to situations outside our immediate concerns. Thus the concept of awareness includes as an inseparable element the sense of social involvement, an empathy with suffering, and a capacity to relate warmly to other people.

For Curle, the self is neither an essentialist substance nor is it defined behavioristically. He conceives of the self in a dynamic way as a process of realization, of becoming, of something to be attained or realized. Education should be a means to promote this self-development, this attainment of awareness. The main issue is whether a higher degree of awareness is intrinsically possible, and whether it is accessible to a greater number of people.

Because of the extroverted traits that characterize much of contemporary Western culture, many people have lost the awareness of the value and necessity of an inner life in depth — an inner life which many rediscover today through an encounter with Eastern religions. The realization of the true self is indeed the key Eastern theme. But an equally fruitful and potentially even richer approach to the growth of awareness lies in the teaching of the Western religious tradition that the human being is created in the image of God. This must not be understood in a static and merely imitative way as if God had simply impressed his image on us like a seal on some plastic material. In a dynamic way, it means that God has raised the human being to a creature which can grow to become the image of God, so that each person, in a completely decisive way, belongs to the self-manifestation of God.

Interpreting the teaching about the image of God in the context of the biblical creation story where it first occurs, many theologians today say that neither man nor woman alone represents this image of God but the image is actualized through their relationship. It is through the cooperation and complementarity of woman and man that the participation in the image of God is developed and deepened. The relationship between the two sexes can be taken here as the basic type of all human relationships, for a person cannot exist without relationships, although these can develop in many different ways. To be a person is to be a center of interpersonal relationships. Thus the image of God lies ultimately in the person as distinguished from a solipsist individual. One might almost say, as far as a human being is born an individual, one is not the image of God; yet as soon as one interrelates with others, one is participating in the image by becoming a person.

In order to relate positively to others, to develop a personal center and self-strength, and to reach higher awareness, the individual needs to exercise self-control, purification, and sometimes even abnegation for the sake of others. These are all part of the "effort" which Teilhard sees as the necessary requirement for the attainment of higher consciousness. This restraint and voluntary self-limitation are also necessary at the level of society. When people like E.F. Schumacher[5] plead for the development of a new lifestyle in international and economic affairs and promote the idea of a necessary and voluntary self-limitation for the sake of international peace and well-being, then this in itself points to a growing awareness at the societal level, an awareness born from the newness of our social situation and the immense crisis facing human society. Schumacher calls the present situation "the end of an era." The refusal on the part of politicians, economists, and scientists to recognize the newness and urgency of the situation is for him "the refusal of consciousness." Contemporary economics, while pretending to be ethically neutral, propagates a philosophy of unlimited expansionism without any regard for the true and genuine needs of human beings, which are limited. Human survival will depend on our ability to overcome this "refusal of consciousness."

When we talk about the individual and society, their conflict or cooperation, this seems an abstract and, to some extent, wrong polarization which leaves out an important link between the two, and that is the family group. In the relationship of the individual to society, the family is an absolutely vital link, for family life is the matrix of all interpersonal relationships. It is a small community where the individual can be firmly rooted and learn to love, a base from which to grow outwards to the larger society and its concerns. The problem is to devise a family structure which will permit the individual a large degree of initiative and freedom, yet assure a proper measure of family cohesion. For the growth of the person and the dynamics of society, this is all-important.

Another aspect worth mentioning is the great number of studies on human aggression. If we wish to enhance the value of human beings as persons and the well-being of society, why do we not study more the truly human capacity to love and to grow through loving in a greater way rather than focussing so exclusively on negative tendencies?

I see the current search for the true value of the human being and for a true community, a new society, together with the concern for interiority, as a universalization of previously specifically religious goals. Thus the religious perspective on the one and the many is not something apart; it is about the very center of the human being. The essence of all religious teaching is always addressed to a person's heart, to the inner being which requires transformation. If this teaching is taken seriously, the required change of heart leads to a new way of relating to oneself and to others; it makes us anew, and by doing so, our relationships and ultimately our society will change. Consequently, if we take the deepest teaching of religion to heart and apply it universally, to individuals and society, something new will emerge. This is not an individualistic spirituality, but

a spirituality with a social dimension. It can only be a hope—
but it may be possible that through such a development the
"refusal of consciousness" may be overcome and the many may
become one.

It would be insufficient to think here of Western religious
teaching alone. The complementarity of thought represented by
different civilizations is aptly expressed by Joseph Needham when
he writes:

> Many Western Europeans and Americans feel themselves the
> representatives of a civilization with a mission to unify the world.
> The civilization of the Occident alone, they think, is universal. This
> is because it is itself united, itself a unity, itself the One capable
> of subsuming all others, the Many. Such pretensions are baseless.[6]

Not only in social action and practice, but also in the realm of
values we have to look for cooperation rather than exclusive
competition. In a crisis of consciousness we cannot afford to be
blind to whatever values we may find. The religious traditions
of humankind are an inspiring source for the reformulation of
values we so urgently need. This is perhaps what Teilhard de
Chardin meant when he said that the era of religion, far from
being bygone, is only just beginning.

## 4

## The Phenomenon of Spirituality

Contemporary philosophers and theologians often concentrate their intellectual efforts on somewhat peripheral questions instead of facing the really big issues relating to the meaning of life today. The philosopher Dorothy Emmet has expressed her concern about this problem by saying:

> Theologians go on increasingly in an ineffectual way. Their ideas are losing their impact, and one no longer feels that there is anything one can *learn* from them. They tend to take refuge in studies of their past history but as *present* thought theology is high and dry, because it is no longer fed by the springs which used to feed it from science, philosophy and the mystical life... The *religious* interest and concern is much more alive..., but it is not met by the ways in which professional philosophers and theologians try to interpret it.[1]

These active religious concerns and interests are often expressed by groups and individuals at the margin of or outside official religious institutions; they are represented by the growth of new spirituality movements, the proliferation of new cults and sects, and a general trend towards religious syncretism. These developments point, in the opinion of more than one observer, to a profound transformation of contemporary religious consciousness. One can notice a growing interest in things spiritual as more people, particularly among the young, are becoming dissatisfied with the affluent consumer society and with the strong alliance between wealth, war, and violence.

Many signs indicate a genuine hunger for things of the mind and spirit, but there also reigns widespread confusion as to what spirituality may mean in concrete terms. What spiritualities are available by way of living examples? What is being offered on the shelves of our bookshops, in the media, in the schools and churches? Many writers on spirituality seem to stress primarily the cultivation of the inner life in a rather evasive way, implying a considerable or even full withdrawal from the contemporary world and its problems, a spirituality little fed by the springs of science, philosophy, and the mystical life of which Dorothy Emmet speaks. It does not seem nearly enough to look for a revival of the spiritual and mystical disciplines of the past, to cultivate the life of prayer, meditation, and worship, or to seek exclusively the resources of inwardness. On the contrary, we need to reconsider the understanding and practice of spirituality *in the light of contemporary experience*, so that we may find practical guidelines to live by in an increasingly complex and confusing world. Not simply guidelines for the individual to pursue an inward spiritual quest, but guidelines to fully participate in the building of secular society in the late twentieth century, guidelines relating to the interdependence of person and community, individual and society, and guidelines to create a truly peaceful world at the global level. Spiritual disciplines must help us to develop integration and wholeness which can truly become the raising leaven of our daily work and world.

In contemporary discussions about spirituality, the reflections of Teilhard de Chardin are given far too little attention. Several writers have examined Teilhard's *own* spirituality,[2] but they have perhaps too exclusively dwelt on his adherence to traditional Christian belief and practice without giving the same close attention to the elements of *newness* contained in his understanding of spirituality, especially the central role that the dynamic of spirituality holds in his analysis of the development of the human phenomenon. Henri de Lubac has probably been most sensitive to this issue, especially in his earlier work *The Religion of Teilhard de Chardin* (1967). Robert Faricy's study *All Things in Christ — Teilhard de Chardin's Spirituality* (1971) does not touch upon two important questions implicit in his title; namely, what are "all things" for us today with our scientific understanding of cosmos and society and the experience of a global world (with the possibility of a planetary civilization and the equal possibility of self-destruction)? Nor does Faricy discuss the new elements in the understanding of Christ based on Teilhard's numerous texts on the cosmic and universal Christ, elements that might provide seeds for further developments in christology. Certainly "all things in Christ" was in one sense as true for Teilhard as it was for St. Paul and countless Christians through the ages, but in another sense, it has become immensely amplified, differentiated, and complexified. Teilhard's own spirituality can perhaps best be summarized as a "cosmic-christic mysticism"[3] or a "pan-christic mysticism." His concrete interweaving of the mystical and the practical, the passive and the active, the theoretical and the applied, throughout the vicissitudes of his own life, can provide an inspiring example for the practice of Christian spirituality in the contemporary world. For this reason, the books on Teilhard's own spirituality can be thought-provoking; they are helpful and necessary, for the inspirational force of his concretely lived example has so far been little explored.

However, we are not so much concerned with this practical aspect as with an attempt to give critical attention to Teilhard's thoughts on spirituality. Much thinking about spirituality might be called "soft thinking" because it is not subjected to either hard analysis or firmly constructed synthesis. It tends to be subjective, individualistic, inspirational, and visionary without having undergone the acid test of critical reflection. Yet in the present state of self-reflective consciousness, this critical test has to be applied, for we live in a period of true crisis demanding decisive choices about future developments regarding the human community and all persons within it.

Teilhard's thinking proceeded from the matrix of mystical experience, without which it cannot be fully understood. But his thinking was equally informed and controlled by the rigorous discipline of scientific training and laborious fieldwork. Such a discipline required the arduous piecing together of fragments of facts to provide evidence for a hypothesis that pushed back the frontiers of our consciousness of the real. The method at work here is a dialectic of analysis and synthesis brought to bear on the entire range of human experience, from the infinitesimally small to the infinitesimally great and the infinitesimally complex. This synthesis of vision unfolds at its most complex and complete in Teilhard's main work, *The Phenomenon of Man*, but it is too complex there, too condensed and abstract, to make all the elements of his argument and analysis fully apparent to the reader. Also, the English title is a mistranslation of the French *Le Phénomène Humain*, for Teilhard speaks about the phenomenon of "man" neither exclusively in a generic sense nor in the restricted sense of the male gender. In his phenomenology based on observation, reflection, and interpretation, he wanted to explore the human phenomenon in all its amplitude from the sources to the summit of its development, as part of the cosmic flux and dynamic of the creative transformation of matter into spirit. Some of our contemporaries find this canvas too large, too complex, and too frightening, fearing as they do that the individual person might be lost to sight in this vast vision of evolutionary development. But Teilhard saw with lucid clarity that it is imperative to ask what it means to be human today, what specifically singles out the *humanum* in the cosmic evolution of life and consciousness.

In his view the evolution of the human phenomenon cannot be dissociated from the phenomenon of religion and mysticism. In fact, he uses the term *mysticism* far more often than the term *spirituality*. This usage is the first hint that a rightly understood and practiced mysticism holds an absolutely central place in his understanding of spirituality. Elements of Teilhard's thought on spirituality are scattered throughout many of his writings. However, they find a particularly clear expresssion in the essays contained in the two volumes *Activation of Energy* (1970) and *Human Energy* (1969). The latter comprises an essay explicitly devoted to the discussion of "The Phenomenon of Spirituality"

(*Human Energy*, pp. 93-112) which we shall use as a basic source to highlight Teilhard's particular understanding of spirituality.

## "THE PHENOMENON OF SPIRITUALITY"

Written in 1937, only a year before he began working on *The Phenomenon of Man*, this essay proposes a *theory* about the phenomenon of the spirit within evolution which to Teilhard appears to be "as *true* as any large scale physical hypothesis can be" (p. 112). "Beside the phenomena of heat, light and the rest studied by physics, there is, just as real and *natural*, the *phenomenon of spirituality*" (p. 93). This is certainly an unusual, if not to say novel, way of looking at spirituality, easily open to criticism from natural scientists, traditional philosophers, and theologians.

The phenomenon of the spirit has always attracted the attention of human beings thinking about themselves, engaged in the exercise of conscious self-reflection. In fact, Teilhard asserts that this phenomenon of spirit

has rightly attracted man's attention more than any other. We are coincidental with it. We feel it from within. It is the very thread of which the other phenomena are woven for us. It is the thing we know best in the world since we are itself, and it is for us everything (p. 93).

Yet Teilhard also points out that, in spite of the natural givenness of "this fundamental element" of the spirit, there seems to exist no adequate understanding as to its nature. In the past, two fundamentally different viewpoints can be discerned. One perspective is represented by all the spiritual philosophies for which spirit is really a "meta-phenomenon," "something so special and so high that it could not possibly be confused with the earthly and material forces which it animates. Incomprehensibly associated with them, it impregnates them but does not mix with them. There is a world of souls and a world of bodies" (p. 93).

In contrast to this, the second perspective, in ascendancy since the nineteenth century but by no means restricted to the modern era, considers the spirit as an "epi-phenomenon," something of secondary and passing importance:

> spirit seems something so small and frail that it becomes accidental and secondary. In face of the vast material energies to which it adds absolutely nothing that can be weighed or measured, the "fact of consciousness" can be regarded as negligible (p. 93).

Teilhard was in no way concerned to distinguish between the many different varieties of spiritualist-idealist philosophies on the one hand and empirical-materialist ones on the other, nor did he inquire into the historical-geographical and social-cultural distribution of these different schools of thought. In a very simple, schematic manner he contrasts these two fundamentally opposite ways of understanding the spirit as either a "meta-phenomenon" or an "epi-phenomenon" with his own understanding which, again, is not unique to him but historically and contemporarily shared by others. He describes this as:

> a third view-point towards which a new physical science and a new philosophy seem to be converging at the present day: that is to say that spirit is neither super-imposed nor accessory to the cosmos, but that it quite simply represents the higher state assumed in and around us by the primal and indefinable thing that we call, for want of a better name, the "stuff of the universe". . . Spirit is neither a meta- nor an epi-phenomenon; it is *the* phenomenon (p. 94).

This passage may be compared with the discussion in *The Phenomenon of Man* where the meaning of the human phenomenon within the process of evolution is presented as *the* phenomenon rather than a meta- or an epi-phenomenon. Regarding the understanding of spirituality, the third perspective presented here is not unlike Teilhard's description of the *via tertia* in his schematic treatment of the different mysticisms.[4] The first, vertical way is the seeking of God to the exclusion of everything else, whether world, work, society, the body. The second way, the horizontal, is the total immersion in the world and its development, in its matter, so to speak, at the loss of any spiritual or transcendent concern. The *via tertia* or third way, by contrast, represents neither a vertical nor a horizontal line but a diagonal one which indicates a basic thrust in spirituality and mysticism whereby spirit comes into being and the spirit of God is found through a creative transformation of matter, world, work, and society.

In a short space the essay "The Phenomenon of Spirituality" demonstrates Teilhard's basic approach, his method of analysis and synthesis, his use of dialectic, as well as his attempt to extend the boundaries of scientific argument by using the concepts and tools of scientific debate for a subject not normally studied within the purview of science. It is for others to consider whether Teilhard's approach remained too "scientistic," too narrowly constrained by the codes of the scientific community of his day, or whether he made a first attempt to explode the all-too-narrow confines of traditional science, an attempt pursued now with much greater thrust and confidence by many more scientists of our own day.

In order to establish the value of his third perspective regarding the phenomenon of spirituality, Teilhard appeals to the argument of "coherence" employed by modern science. He wishes to establish the truth of his thesis about spirituality by trying to show that his viewpoint more coherently organizes or harmonizes a larger body of facts regarding our experience, thoughts, and actions in the contemporary world.

The evidence for this argument is tightly structured under the three headings of "Spiritualization," "Personalization," and "Moral Application." It would be too long to analyze his argument step by step, but I would like to pick out the salient features of each section. In "Spiritualization" he emphasizes the cosmic roots and dimensions of the spirit. Taken as a whole, the dimensions of the spirit "are dimensions of the universe itself" (p. 95) and "the phenomenon of the spirit is coextensive with the very evolution of the earth" (p. 98). Contrary to the customary ways of looking at spirit and spirituality primarily from an individual and personal point of view, Teilhard first assumes a cosmic and collective perspective, emphasizing their global dimension. For him, "the phenomenon of spirit is not a divided mass; it displays a general manner of being, a collective state peculiar to our world" which is defined by a certain tension of consciousness on the surface of the earth, an "animated covering of our planet" for which Teilhard coined the term *noosphere.* The phenomenon of the spirit has to be examined within a time perspective, in terms of its past, present, and future. In other words, the phenomenon of spirit is linked to growth in complexity and consciousness; it is affected by a profound dynamic and a process of transformation. For Teilhard, the true name for spirit is *spiritualization,* a dynamic process linked to increasing interiorization, the growth of consciousness in its movement from the unconscious to the conscious, and from the conscious to the self-conscious, leading to a "cosmic *change of state*" (p. 97). Teilhard believes that this perspective allows him to link the evolution of spirit and matter in such a way that it overcomes their traditional contradictions, stressed in an exclusive way by either materialists or spiritualists.

The growth of spirit is linked to the historical expansion of consciousness on earth as well as to its increased concentration or "interiorization" within the individual person. Thus, at its most intimate, it is linked with a process of personalization to which the second part of the essay is devoted. In this densely packed section, Teilhard's thoughts about the process of centering, the image of the center and the sphere, and his philosophy of creative union through the unification of multiple elements into a complex All which is a person, are all briefly alluded to. "The phenomenon of spirit has entered into a higher and decisive phase by becoming the phenomenon of man" (p. 102). Looked at phenomenologically, we encounter a vast pluralism in the world around us, characterized by various forms or elements of consciousness (or unconsciousness). The question now arises how to understand and interpret the existence of this plurality and fragmentation. Was there a primal unity of things, one reality which has been broken up into fragmentary consciousness*es* or, on the contrary, can we imagine that these elements will "join other like fragments in the building of a super-consciousness" (p. 103)? Teilhard adopts the latter point of view. He sees the center of a person being enhanced through union with others. This process of unification and convergence culminates in union with the spirit of God or the All, elsewhere also called Christ Omega. Here he simply states:

> As regards the final nature of the spirit into which all spirituality converges, that is to say all the personality in the world, we see that its supreme simplicity contains a prodigious complexity. In that spirit . . . all the elements into which the personal consciousness of the world appeared in the beginning to be broken up . . . are carried to their maximum individual differentiation by maximum union with the All . . .
>
> As regards the direction of our present activity, we observe that, to complete ourselves, we must pass into a greater than ourselves. Survival and also "super-life" await us in the direction of a growing consciousness and love of the universal. All our action should be organized — that is to say our morality should be shaped — towards reaching (and at the same time bringing into being) this pole (p. 105).

The third section, entitled "Moral Application," tries to spell out some of the implications of this perspective. Here Teilhard contrasts the old "morality of balance" with a new "morality of movement." Instead of being a jurist trying to preserve and protect the individual and the balance of society, the moralist should become "the technician and engineer of the spiritual energies of the world," whose task is "to develop, by awakening and convergence, the individual riches of the earth" (p.106).

Teilhard speaks of "the present crisis in morality" (p. 110). While deliberately refraining from "a critique of religions," he emphasizes that it is necessary for the religions to change in order to meet the new needs of today (p. 110). Again in summary form he lists three principles which define the value of human action according to a morality of movement. He writes:

i. *Only* finally good is what makes for the growth of the spirit on earth.

ii. Good (at least basically and partially) is *everything* that brings a spiritual growth to the world.

iii. Finally *best* is what assures their highest development to the spiritual powers of the earth (p. 107 f.).

He applies these principles to a number of examples, especially money morality and the morality of love. The morality of balance is characterized as a "closed morality," whereas the morality of movement is an "open morality" inclined towards the future, in the direction of greater consciousness, and ultimately in pursuit of a God conceived as a God of cosmic synthesis as well as a supremely personal God. The cosmic genesis of the spirit (he describes "the development of consciousness as *the* essential phenomenon of nature," p. 105) is linked to "a God to be realized by effort, and yet a personal God to be submitted to in love" (p. 109). "The time has passed in which God could simply impose Himself on us from without, as master and owner of the estate. Henceforth the world will only kneel before the organic centre of its evolution" (p. 110).

Thus the morality of movement modifies or rather completes our ideas of goodness and perfection. Teilhard speaks of the "powerlessness of moralities of balance to govern the earth," the vain attempt "to maintain social and international order by the limitation of force." What we need is a change of state, a morality of movement and love, a "transformation which will bring the universe from the material to the spiritual state" (p. 112). In fact, "What we are all more or less lacking at this moment is a new definition of holiness" (p. 110).

Teilhard is surely not alone in saying this, but he said it earlier than most. He reflected about spirituality both in theory and practice, yet his complex and rich thought is at times clothed in such abstract, if not lifeless, language, possessing all the dryness of a scientific memoir, that it is difficult for many readers to see what he wants to say.

His ideas about the growth of the spirit and the phenomenon of spirituality in the development of the world are presented as a hypothesis, a theory. The hypothesis of a cosmos "in spiritual transformation" (p. 110) explains for him best of all the features and behavior of the world around us. But beyond the explanatory power of this theory he also thinks that further proof for it can be obtained by direct observation. This proof is available in the experience of the mystics and their love of God. Without further analysis, his essay simply concludes with the assertion:

> If it is true, as we have been led to imagine, that cosmic developments of consciousness depend on the existence of a higher and independent centre of personality, there must be a means without leaving the empirical field, of recognizing around us, in the personalized zones of the universe, some psychic effect (radiation or attraction) specifically connected with the operation of this centre, and consequently revealing its positive existence.
>
> The definitive discovery of the phenomenon of the spirit is bound up with the analysis (which science will one day finally undertake) of the "mystical phenomenon," that is of the love of God (p. 112).

This is an important essay, especially when one considers that it was written over fifty years ago. Yet it has not been given the attention it deserves.[5] From the perspective of contemporary thinking about spirituality, one can single out significant elements in Teilhard's understanding and relate them to practical considerations. Within an overall evolutionary approach the dynamic, process-character of spirituality as growing spiritualization in both the individual and society provides the basic framework for his thinking. Within this framework, three interrelating perspectives can help us to situate the practice of spirituality: 1) spirituality and time; 2) spirituality and energy; 3) spirituality and development.

## 1. Spirituality and Time

Teilhard's thinking is shaped by the dynamic of the time-process and the directionality of time moving from the past to the future. In this perspective more emphasis is placed on the potential of development than on the question of origin. There is also a sharp awareness of the acceleration of time, clearly apparent in the increase of inventions and social changes and the intensification of shared thinking made possible through the growth in communications. Unlike some authors who consider spirituality as operating in a timeless perspective, being essentially of the same kind and quality at all times and places, Teilhard saw the modern experience of time as itself affecting the practice of spirituality. Thus, a revival of past spiritualities, whether Christian, Buddhist or Islamic, which is not also a new creation, will not be enough. Spirituality must neither be time- nor place-evasive by divorcing itself through segregation and contemplation from the problems of the "real world." To be involved in true "soul-making," to use an expression of Keats, the knowledge, experience, and sensibility of our age have to be taken into account. Certain writers, and also certain spiritual traditions, consider the spiritual quest as something which concerns only the individual and his or her self-realization.[6] For Teilhard, on the contrary, the problem of spirituality is linked not only to the stages of the life-cycle development of the individual psyche, but also to the evolution of society and humankind as a whole. Spirituality is a phenomenon of universal extension closely interwoven with the development of the human phenomenon in all its amplitude. In other words, the evolution of consciousness, of social structure, and of spirituality are closely interrelated.

It is a vain effort to think that past spiritualities can be transplanted across time and cultures without being changed in the process, or without being affected by the complexification of contemporary social developments and thinking. Teilhard felt that we are at a new critical threshold in the development of human evolution, a breakthrough from the individual to a social phase of consciousness. The American theologian Ewert H. Cousins has called this "the second axial period" after Jaspers' term "the first axial period."[7] Whereas the first period, between the sixth and fifth centuries B.C.E., produced a breakthrough to individual, self-reflective consciousness, this second axial period is characterized by the emergence of global consciousness. Cousins understands this global development in two senses: it is global in that it encompasses the entire human community and all its historical experience around the globe; it is also global in that it is a consciousness recovering its rootedness in the earth. Teilhard fully valued the human being's rootedness in nature; he also stressed the urgency of moral choices for building the human community now, so as not to let its developments run riot and thereby destroy life on our planet.

## 2. Spirituality and Energy

Thinking about the future of human development, Teilhard was at an early stage conscious of the problem of energy resources, but conceived of it in much wider terms than usually understood. He expressed his surprise and concern over the fact that many thousands of engineers, scientists, and technicians are preoccupied with the available quantity of the world's material energy resources, its stocks of coal, oil, and uranium, whereas no one seems to worry about the availability of spiritual, moral, mental, and psychic energy resources, which supply the deepest springs for human action. Who surveys and takes stock of these resources, who cares to feed our "zest for life," to animate our taste for growth and development, our need for action, so that we shall not succumb to the very real danger of indifference, boredom, and the lack of a love for life?

Teilhard considered that the world religions possessed irreplaceable spiritual energy resources, but he did not divorce their spiritualities from concrete material and social development. In terms of our material culture, our technological and scientific know-how, we can to some extent already see a global oneness of external civilization, but the forces of external unification alone are not enough. Most of all we need a common mind and spirit which can weld humankind into a more closely knit community. Teilhard saw the forces of convergence, of coming more closely together, clearly at work in the realm of material and social developments. He linked these developments with the convergence of world religions and their distinct spiritualities. Convergence is not an automatic process, however; it requires critical reflection, decisive moral choices and definite action. Although Teilhard looked at the different spiritualities only in a very schematic, one might even say superficial, way, he stressed the need to approach the problem of spirituality today in a *global, cross-cultural,* and *convergent* perspective, whereby Western and Eastern religions have to come into much closer contact. What is called interreligious encounter or dialogue must not be limited to getting to know one another or remaining at the simple level of sharing one's experiences. Convergence also requires a process of mutual critical reflection which can act as a catalyst by bringing out the distinctive element of each religious tradition within a global religious heritage. Theologically, very little detailed work has been done on the convergence of religious and spiritual traditions.[8] Much that is being published on the encounter of religions belongs to a naively syncretistic perspective without looking at spiritual energy resources in terms of globally convergent developments. Several writers have praised the creative originality of Teilhard's views of convergence. Yet in the light of contemporary experience, their limitations have to be pointed out, too, as Ewert Cousins has done:

> Although Teilhard provided a brilliant theory for understanding the convergence of religions, I believe that his own application of the theory to specific religions was limited. In his personal reaction to the religions he encountered in the Orient and in his theoretical speculations on them, he seems to lack the very complexification of consciousness that is characteristic of this period in the evolution of religious consciousness. I believe that the central element in this new complexified religious consciousness is sympathy or empathy for the values of other religions. For example, the Christian does not look on the other religion merely from his own theological perspective; rather he enters into the very structure of consciousness of the other religion and grasps its distinctive values from *its* own perspective. From this perspective he also views his own tradition, both sympathetically and critically. Then he returns to his Christian consciousness, but now enriched by his own horizons and with the spiritual energies that he has activated by a center-to-center union with the other mode of consciousness. In the present generation of Christian theologians, this empathetic religious consciousness is appearing in a way not found in Teilhard himself or the theologians of his time.[9]

Teilhard emphasized that the most powerful energy for the unification of the human community and the centering of the individual person is the energy of love. Love has its roots in cosmic evolution, but it ascends to the summit of the spirit. It is the "unitive element" which brings everything together from the smallest "within" in matter to the highest personal union. Teilhard tried to trace the evolution of love. He saw it as an all-pervading cosmic principle, an untamed force which has its roots deep in matter; its matrix is both the earth and the body. Thus, human sexuality is one of the most powerful forces to shape, and also to distort, human experience. All too often, spirituality has been pursued in separation from and in denial of sexuality, whereas Teilhard stresses the need for the transformation and sublimation of the powers of sexuality. The human sense of the earth and the sense of the body are not divorced from the sense and experience of the spirit. From its roots in the earth and the body, love can lead to the height and transcendence of the spirit, and therefore love is our most sacred energy resource, the very lifeblood of further human spiritual evolution.

### 3. Spirituality and Development

Teilhard's ideas about the concrete role and power of the energies of love are central to his understanding of the human phenomenon and the place of spirituality within it. Another name for evolution at the social level is development, but all too often development is seen only as an economic problem, or as a problem of wealth and justice, the distribution of resources and the balance of power. Teilhard's inspiring words about "building the earth" can provide a strong inspirational force for this kind of development, but his question about the spiritual energy resources available today and his vision of the convergence of spiritualities also pose the question of how far we have thought about the spiritual dimensions of development. How far may the question of the inner development of human beings also become an issue of justice and concern for us in the future? The Russian philosopher Berdyayev rightly pointed out long ago that the problem of labor and of industrial relations in modern society has so far not been tackled by traditional spirituality nor, as mentioned before, has the problem of sexual activity within the context of current developments in medicine and genetics. Berdyayev describes the revival of inwardness as a truly revolutionary act in relationship to the outer world; it may prove to be a revolt against determinism, a spiritual permeation of the world which will transfigure it. But this would not be achieved by a withdrawal into inwardness alone without paying full attention to the requirements of the developments of society. If we were truly able to creatively combine the contemplative and the active modes, not in terms of the separation of people, but in terms of alternating phases in the daily rhythm of our lives, if we could learn to combine the spiritual insights of the mystics with full participation in secular society, perhaps this would truly be the birth of a new religion, the development of Christianity to its limits and beyond itself, the development of what Teilhard also called "a new mysticism," a mysticism of action which would give us that new understanding of holiness so much needed today.

When Teilhard reflected on the evolution of spirituality, he was in search of a force of integration, a spirituality that can creatively relate the different aspects of reality and experience to each other rather than separate and divide them into dichotomies of spirit/matter, mind/body, heaven/earth, East/West, etc.[10] From the vantage point of our own day, which has experienced further inner and outer developments, we can see the particular constraints of the situation from which Teilhard was speaking—as an exile in the Far East living at the margin of new developments, as a censured priest living in the closed atmosphere of the pre-Council Roman Church, as a European living among colonial expatriates in the Far East, as a Western Christian looking at Eastern religions from the outside rather than the inside.

But Teilhard tried more than most to develop a balanced, holistic spirituality relating to global concerns. Within the cosmic emergence of the human phenomenon, the genesis and rise of the spirit takes a very special place. Analyzing the structural relationship between spirit and matter, he emphasized the preeminence and sovereignty of the spirit, pointing to its growth and transformation as well as its transformative powers in building up and creating one earth. Drawing on powerful symbols and formative personal experiences, he saw that ˹the center of spirituality must be animated by the dynamics of love. The traditional concept of love is too static, too "spiritualized" and divorced from natural passion in which all love, including the love of God, must be rooted. Teilhard spoke of "the transformation of love," whereby love is undergoing a change of state. This love is the only energy capable of transforming human society. Towards the end of his life he was fascinated with developing a comprehensive program for the study of "human energetics" closely related to what he once described as his particular vocation, namely, "the strategic defense of the noosphere." Probing the full meaning of this new word of Teilhard's, one must remember that the noosphere, the specifically human layer covering the earth, is not only a sphere of conscious reflection and invention, but also the sphere of union between souls, the sphere of true love. It is interesting to note that the Greek *noùs*, on which *noosphere* is based, does not denote the ordinary mind with its faculty of reasoning, but a faculty of direct, intuitive vision, a spiritual faculty which in its *noèsis* transcends the multiplicity of discursive reasoning and overcomes the subject-object differentiation in a vision of unity. For the Greeks, the *noùs* was the spiritual intellect, which primarily serves as the instrument of self-transcendence. Given this etymology of the term *noùs*, one can immediately see that we have to go further than analytical-critical reflection in our understanding of the noosphere. The growth of the noosphere is closely related to the rise and expansion of consciousness, but at the center and heart of the noosphere, at the center of the human, lies the radically transforming power of spirituality with the source of all energy residing in the fire of love and union. This fire is burning most vividly in the life of the mystics and saints, the seers of all ages and climes. Teilhard strongly criticized a one-sided, evasive mysticism, but, rightly understood, the mystic is the true animator of the world:

> Seeing the mystic immobile, crucified or rapt in prayer, some may perhaps think that his activity is in abeyance or has left this earth: they are mistaken. Nothing in the world is more intensely alive

# Mysticism and Contemporary Society

Patrick Grant, in his book *Literature of Mysticism in Western Tradition* (1983), claims that mysticism cannot be discussed separately from a framework of faith. He concludes his reflections on the interrelationship between "Mysticism, Faith and Culture" with an additional suggestion:

> If the *via mystica* is to be expressed in language, the language of poetry is the most complete, most satisfactory, analogue for the delicate equilibrium of faith and personal experience lived in the context of a culture both nourishing and testing. Those that have ears to hear, let them hear, for "Those who love the world indeed know the words or verses of our songs, but not their music."[1]

Grant approaches mysticism from the background of a scholar in English literature, but there are many other perspectives in the current study of mysticism.[2] The secondary literature on mysticism has grown to extraordinary proportions over the last two decades or so, and many are the editions of texts by mystics from different religious traditions. The important contributions to the two volumes edited by Steven T. Katz, *Mysticism and Philosophical Analysis* (1978)[3] and *Mysticism and Religious Traditions* (1983)[4] express the general tendency to recognize the pluralism of mystical experience and analyze its occurrence in a wider social, psychological, linguistic, philosophical, and theological context.

One could undertake a study of the contemporary study of mysticism, and there are already a number of publications primarily concerned with this meta-level rather than with mysticism itself. One can ask what this may possibly tell us about contemporary society, or, alternatively, what significance this growing interest in mysticism may have for the present and future of Western and possibly global society. In all this fast-growing body of literature, apart from a few occasional references, there hardly ever seems to be any mention nor any sustained critical discussion of the French mystic and scientist Pierre Teilhard de Chardin (1881-1955), his challenging reflections on mysticism, and its importance for contemporary society. I shall briefly outline Teilhard's thought on mysticism (1), then highlight specific features of his "mysticism of action" in relationship to other aspects of his thought (2), and finally, relate my remarks to reflections on contemporary society (3).

## 1. Teilhard's Thought on Mysticism

Teilhard de Chardin assigns a central place to religion, especially to mysticism, in the ongoing development of humankind. The primary matrix for his understanding of mysticism was provided by his own experience. Autobiographical references in his works point to a deep unity of life and thought and refer to certain formative mystical experiences which structured what he called his "fundamental vision."[5] The indispensable key for unlocking this experiential and mystical quality of his work is the late essay "The Heart of Matter" (1950),[6] a brief spiritual autobiography. A further elaboration and moving expression of this mystical vision of the world is found in "The Christic" (1955),[7] completed shortly before his death.

However, there are many clues in earlier essays, diaries, and letters. His earliest attempt to describe his spiritual development goes back as far as 1918 when, in the essay "*Mon Univers*,"[8] he outlined several elements of his mystical experience and vision.

The experience came first; it provided the nucleus from which he developed a philosophy, a theology, and an integral worldview which included an interpretation of mysticism which comprised a partly new understanding of spirituality. This primacy of experience is also emphasized in an early diary entry which reads: "The true interest of life does not lie in discovery and knowledge—but in *realization*..."[9]

In the early essays in *Writings in Time of War*,[10] Teilhard frequently refers to the experience of the mystic seer, the "voyant" whose vision constructs the world anew: he experiences and sees something new he wants to communicate to others. What did Teilhard see and what did he want to say?

The unfolding of his vision is vividly described in "The Heart of Matter" (1950). From earliest childhood he had certain decisive experiences which made him seek something absolute, permanent, and everlasting which was at the same time tangible and concrete. At first, this search expressed itself in a passion for collecting rocks and stones; later, it was the contact with nature on a grander scale, further intensified through his scientific interests and studies. This was initially kindled by his father, whereas the development of his religious views owed much to his mother, whose faith was steeped in the Christian mystics.

As a child and young man, Teilhard had several mystical experiences which he described later as a realization of cosmic consciousness. When he was able to articulate these experiences, he became fully aware that all he could ever write was only a feeble echo of what he had lived and felt with such intensity. The experience of the fundamental oneness, beauty, and divine quality of nature revealed a monistic and pantheistic inclination, a nature mysticism which was to remain with him all his life, although it underwent several important modifications.

During his years of studying theology in England (Hastings, 1908-12), his strong attraction to nature grew more intensive through his discovery of the full meaning of evolution. The full realization of the importance of evolution became central both for his approach to the cosmos and for the reinterpretation of his religious beliefs, particularly his understanding of Christ. The cosmic and christic sense, which he later described as the two sides of his being, converged into a powerful vision of the universal and cosmic Christ, a symbol of great integrative force.[11] It is a vision that remains inseparable from the mystical quality of his nature experiences, but the monistic pantheism of earlier years had gradually been prolonged and transcended into what he occasionally referred to as "pan-Christic monism,"[12] and what might also be called a person-centered theistic mysticism or pantheism.

A further formative experience is related to his contact with the East, especially his long stay in China. Teilhard unequivocally stated in "The Heart of Matter" that his pan-christic mysticism matured "in the two great atmospheres of Asia and the War."[13] These two experiences were complementary and found their final expression in two of his most important writings on spirituality, *The Mass on the World* (1923) and *The Divine Milieu* (1927).

China eventually became the major field of his professional scientific activity (1926-46) and deeply influenced his thinking. The experience of China revealed to him the immensity of the earth and its peoples. He later judged the invitation to come to China as "the decisive event of his destiny."[14] Without it he would not have developed his vision of convergent unity and synthesis the way he did. This is as true of his understanding of religion and mysticism as it is of other aspects of his work.

His many essays express the fundamental continuity and coherence of a mystical vision over a lifetime. Given the need to interpret these experiences to himself and others, he inquired into the phenomenon of mysticism inside and outside Christianity. Comparisons with the experiences of other mystics were initially personally motivated; they were undertaken to illuminate or explicate his own, and this accounts for some of the limitations of his approach.

Many commentators have recognized the mystical quest of Teilhard's life. But whereas his Christ-centered mysticism has been frequently discussed, his typological interpretation and emphasis on the importance of mysticism for the future of religion and society have received far less attention. There has also been an overriding tendency to interpret Teilhard's general worldview, centered on the emergence of the "noosphere" and his understanding of mysticism, in an exclusively intellectualist manner. He himself objected to this interpretation, for the "fundamental harmony of the universe" he felt and the integral vision he perceived, could not be easily expressed by words, but was more like a quality or taste to be perceived. Few people know the passage written to Ida Treat in February 1927: "Those who do not hear the fundamental harmony of the Universe which I try to transcribe (fortunately, many do) look in what I write for some kind of narrowly logical system, and are confused or angry. Fundamentally, it is not possible to transmit directly by words the perception of a quality, a taste. Once again, it would be more to my purpose to be a shadow of Wagner than a shadow of Darwin. Taking myself as I am, I see no better course than to strive by all means to reveal Humanity to Men."[15]

From early on Teilhard objected to a narrow definition of mysticism. He uses the word *mysticism* in a comprehensive sense and does not restrict it to extraordinary contemplative or unitive experiences only. On one hand, he links *mysticism* to a continuum of progressively more "centered" experiences, ranging from pantheistic to monistic to theistic forms; on the other hand, *mysticism* stands for the goal of all spiritual life and becomes synonymous with the deepest layer of human spirituality. This can only be realized by integrating a person's outer activities with the inner life of the spirit, centered in the dynamic powers of love. He criticized Christian theology for its tendency "to give the word *mystical* a minimum of organic or physical meaning." This is due to "the very common mistake of regarding the spiritual as an attenuation of the material, whereas it is in fact the material carried beyond itself: it is super-material."[16] He also referred to "the vast and polymorphous domain of mysticism."[17] It was his comparatively wide reading which, more than his own experience, made him aware of the variety of phenomena designated by the term *mysticism.* But Teilhard did not argue for a sharp break between natural pantheism on one hand and religious mysticism of a monistic, or theistic, kind on the other. He saw these different experiences as continuous and organically interrelated although each possesses a distinctive element of its own.

Structurally and ontologically, Teilhard always distinguished between two basic types of mysticism as fundamental alternatives or even opposites. His terminology is inconsistent and rather fluid, yet whatever the terms used, the polarity is always clearly present. The two basic types of mysticism are described as "two solutions to the problem of the one and the many" (1931), "two roads of spiritualization" (1932), "two converse forms of the spirit" (1950), or "two principal ways tried by the mystics" (1951). Although this changing terminology is confusing, a comparative analysis of Teilhard's writings reveals certain common features of his typological interpretation of mysticism.

Different types of mysticism are often distinguished on the basis of whether fundamentally unitive experiences are understood as absorption into, or union with, the Absolute. Teilhard hinges his distinction of two basic types of mysticism on the *process of unification.* The very choice of the word *unification* implies that it is not simply a question of the union of two given terms, the human person and the Absolute, but a dynamic process of successive "centering." This involves the inner unification or integration of the self as well as the outer unification of what surrounds the human being, i.e., other people as well as work and nature. This process of unification has such central importance in his worldview that it is sharply set off from any mysticism of identification which, in his view, was traditionally mainly prevalent in the East, and is summarily and quite wrongly referred to as the "road of the East."

There are many texts which express the fundamental distinction of these two basic types of mysticism. A succinct summary is found in "Some Notes on the Mystical Sense: An Attempt at Clarification" (1951).[18] The first type, a "*mysticism of identification,*" implies an identification of man, "of each and all," with an undifferentiated common ground. It means the fusion or dissolution of human specificity, represented by personal consciousness, with an "ineffable of de-differentiation and de-personalization." Because of the negation of the central core of personhood, both in the Absolute and in human experience, this is "by definition and by structure" a "mysticism WITHOUT LOVE."

The second type is a "*mysticism of unification.*" Instead of dissolution and fusion, it is the concentration and unification of each and all "through a peak of intensity arrived at by what is most incommunicable in each element." Although not specifically mentioned, personhood and its ultimate fulfillment in a higher personal center are central to this second type. This type of mysticism represents "an ultra-personalizing, ultra-determining, and ultra-differentiating UNIFICATION of the elements within a common focus; the specific effect of LOVE."

The main difference, then, between a *mysticism of identification* and a *mysticism of unification* is the absence or presence of personal love, itself dependent on a specific understanding of the personal nature of the human being and the Absolute. It must be stressed that Teilhard's basic typology must not be understood to simply reiterate the distinction between a monistic and a theistic type of mysticism. The presence of personal love in this context implies more than a loving relationship of union between us and God. It means more than a simple coming together, for it includes, at the same time, a complex and increasingly convergent process of unification. Thus, the meaning of love itself is altered through being understood in a much more dynamic sense.[19] Even when Teilhard refers elsewhere simply to "union" or "unity," he still associates the idea of unification with these terms.

The second type of mysticism — that of unification — is not strictly identical with theistic forms of mysticism. Instead, it is "a road not yet described in any 'book' (?!). . . the true path 'towards and for' oneness."[20] It is also designated as the new "road of the West," a path of unification which has become possible through the contact of Christianity with the modern world. The two basic "ways" of mysticism are distinguished by the absence or presence of love in an *ultra*personal God. The first type is, then, an essentially monistic mysticism; the second a *trans-theistic mysticism* to which Christianity tends but which has not yet been fully worked out. Structurally, through its theology, and practically through the emphasis given to love, Christianity belongs to the second type. Yet the mysticism of the past shows a certain "lack of richness"; it is "not sufficiently universalist and cosmic," for oneness was too exclusively sought "in *singleness,* rather than in God's *synthetic power*". God was loved "*above* all things" rather than "*in* and *through* all things."[21]

Other texts emphasize less the process of unification as opposed to identification than a basic polarity expressed through a predominantly forward or upward orientation. The inherent tension of these two orientations is transcended through a third direction representing a new synthesis. Diagrammatically this can be shown in the following way:

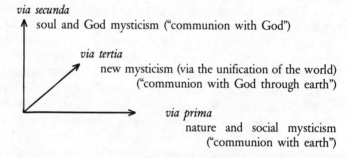

*via secunda*
soul and God mysticism ("communion with God")

*via tertia*
new mysticism (via the unification of the world)
("communion with God through earth")

*via prima*
nature and social mysticism
("communion with earth")

The horizontal line stands for pantheistic nature mysticism and a social mysticism of the collective, represented by various forms of neo-humanism. This mysticism of the world is the *via prima*, opposed to the vertical line of the *via secunda*, the way of all traditional mysticism, which seeks to link us directly with the Absolute to the exclusion of the world (i.e., all forms of either soul or God mysticism). The diagonal *via tertia* indicates the emergence of a new kind of mysticism whereby the human being is united with the Absolute *via the unification of the world.*[22]

This diagram is a schematic representation of what might be called the recurrent *leitmotif* of Teilhard's entire work, first expressed in the motto of "Cosmic Life" (1916): "There is a communion with God, and a communion with earth, and a communion with God through earth."[23] The "communion with earth" initially refers to the experience of monistic pantheism, but later it stands for *any* merely immanent or inner-worldly attitude. "Communion with God" stands for an excessively other-worldly attitude, an understanding of God and religion as separate from the world. The exclusive concern for a transcendent reality, often regarded as the main characteristic of the religious quest, does not place enough importance on the value of human effort and the development of the world, the building of the earth. The two attitudes—"communion with earth" and "communion with God"—are regarded as incomplete and deficient. What is sought is a "communion with God through earth" or a new synthesis where the religious and mystical are closely interdependent with the experience of the natural world and the construction of the social world.

## 2. Significant Features of Teilhard's Mysticism of Action

Teilhard understood the search for unification via the tangible as a fundamentally Western preoccupation. The concern for the value of the material world is closely rooted in the Christian understanding of the Incarnation. Yet the full implications of an incarnational approach, i.e., the transformation and sanctification of all human and earthly realities, take on an altogether different dimension with the relatively modern discovery and analysis of what these realities in themselves are. With advancing knowledge, the limits of the real are forever further pushed back; the world surrounding us expands its parameter. For Teilhard, the search for unitary knowledge in the scientific domain is closely related to man's mystic search in the religious domain.

This interrelated quest for oneness made him speak of a "new mysticism" where unity is achieved through ultradifferentiation. Many passages could be quoted where the idea of a new "mysticism of evolution," a "mysticism of action," is expressed, suggesting a new vision related to the development of a new world. Teilhard's understanding of mysticism cannot be solely assessed by reference to the mystics of the past; his interpretation of mysticism is strongly future-oriented and is also basically *evaluative*. The *mysticism of identification* and that of *unification* are not simple equivalents, but one type is seen as more developed, fuller, richer, truer. Many passages indicate this evaluative perspective. For example, Teilhard is reported to have said at a meeting of the French branch of the World Congress of Faiths, whose activities he strongly supported:

I believe the mystical is less different, less separated from the rational than one says, but I finally also believe that the whole problem which the world, and we in particular, are presently facing, is a problem of faith... I have the weakness to believe that the West has a very strong latent mysticism, underlying, not made explicit yet, but at least as strong as Eastern mysticism. If the western group were really able to express in a new manner, or to renew the mysticism of the West of which I once spoke, I think that would be something much more powerful than even dialogue, for it would make a faith appear within mankind, a mysticism which does not yet exist.[24]

Teilhard primarily sought a new formulation for a mysticism of the West, that is to say, a mysticism rooted in the Christian doctrines of creation and incarnation, but expressed in a new manner. Whereas in his earlier years he presented Christianity as "the very religion of evolution,"[25] he later increasingly stressed the need for a deep transformation of his own religious tradition:

Christianity has only a chance to survive... if it shows itself capable... to activate to a maximum in man "the energy of self-evolution," i.e., if it is successful... not only in "amorising" the world but in valuing it more highly than any other form of religion.[26]

What is needed is no longer simply a "Christianity faithfully extended to its utmost limit,"[27] but a "Christianity which surpasses itself,"[28] the emergence of something "trans-Christian" in theology and mysticism.[29] It was in this sense that he talked about "the urgent need for the formulation of a mysticism of the West,"[30] a "new mysticism, at once fully human and fully Christian" which could be the source of a new energy for which "we have as yet *no name!*"[31] Christian love is given a decisive place in his interpretation of mysticism, but it is also stressed that this love — identified as the "Christian mystical act" *par excellence* — has not yet found its fullest expression, that is to say, it has to grow further and become more universalized.[32]

All these formulations indicate suggestions and explorations in need of further development. Weighing up different texts, particularly those of later years, one realizes Teilhard's awareness of the necessary, in fact, essential contribution of Eastern religious insights to a newly emerging mysticism which, instead of being merely a mysticism of the West, represents, in fact, a "new mysticism of convergence."[33] The growing convergence of world religions is of great importance in this respect. Although the encounter of religions and theological reflections on interreligious dialogue have by now progressed beyond what Teilhard himself knew and thought, his ideas on the convergence of religions still provide stimulating reading but cannot be discussed here.[34]

Teilhard's thoughts on mysticism are based on the premise that the spiritual quest of human beings is not perennially the same. A change in human consciousness and self-understanding, linked to new historical and social developments, has brought about a situation where spiritual needs have come into sharper focus. The closer coming together of humankind observable in many areas of human endeavor requires a new approach to the understanding and practice of spirituality. It is this need, born from a historically new situation, which Teilhard saw and felt with an extraordinary depth and intensity unlike few others. Based on formative mystical experiences and a lifelong reflection on the meaning of mysticism, he put forward a particular interpretation which diverges from that of other writers in several respects.

An important aspect of his interpretation of mysticism lies in the fact that, in his view, the integration of the inner self and the search for the Absolute do not occur independently from time. Given modern developments, an adequate religious worldview for the present and the future cannot be entirely modelled on patterns of the past. To seek ultimate unity implies at the same time a changed relationship between the human being and all other phenomena in the world; thus, it must be accompanied by a process of unification. Consequently, the interpretation of mysticism is closely linked to a new emphasis on the importance of human action. It is, in fact, in and through action that the spirit unfolds and that spirituality grows. Spirituality is no longer simply a problem of inwardness, as in the mysticism of the past. On the contrary, the problem of human action, together with the choice of the right values and beliefs on which to base such action, is the major problem of the spirit today.

This fundamental stress on the newness of present time ultimately overcomes and transcends the past divisions in space, linked to separate religious developments in East and West. What can the religious teachings of the past, whether Eastern or Western, contribute to the "building of the earth," to the shaping of the future? What general structures can be discerned in the mysticism of the past? And how far are these relevant or redundant for contemporary spirituality? These were some of the main questions motivating his inquiry into the nature of mysticism. Moved by these questions, Teilhard looked for the active and animating elements in different religious traditions, for pointers towards a new religious breakthrough, and for a yet unformulated new mysticism.

Teilhard evaluated religious and mystical traditions according to their capacity to supply the deepest sources of energy for human action. In the last years of his life, he was particularly concerned with developing a "science of human energetics."[35] He understood this as a systematic study of the required energy for the further self-evolution of humankind. While his general understanding of energy in evolution has been studied in some detail, the central role of the forces of religion and mysticism for this "energetics" has so far received little attention. It is in fact the conjunction of religion, science, and mysticism[36] which is central to Teilhard's vision of the human phenomenon. He referred to the necessary encounter of physics or sciences in general with mysticism in "an evolutionary energetics."[37] Such an "energetics" alone, rather than traditional metaphysics, is capable of defining the necessary conditions of culture, morality, and religion.[38]

Ultimately, Teilhard looked for unity, homogeneity, and a final coherence of the mystical vison in the light of modern science, relating religious awareness to the development of modern consciousness. Although science cannot determine our image of God, given the course of its growth, it nevertheless rules out certain approaches to the Absolute and to worship.[39]

For the religions of the past "the problem of human progress (as we understand it today) *did not arise*,"[40] but this problem is assuming ever greater urgency today. It is linked to the development of modern science and technology, frequently misunderstood as something merely external, and even more to a progressive change in human consciousness, individual as well as social, to what Teilhard calls the rise of the "noosphere."

Religious teaching and practice must meaningfully relate to contemporary society's most urgent task of "building the earth" and shaping the future. Thus, the way of mysticism must be linked to social and practical life, providing a spirituality which animates and activates human beings to cope with the world rather than to inwardly escape from it.

This search for a harmonious balance between the unification of the world and a person's inner life introduces an element of newness into the understanding of mysticism and includes aspects usually thought of as separate. Mysticism is no longer primarily the pursuit of contemplatives, open only to monastics and ascetics, but an experience potentially open to all. It is closely connected with people's attitude to the natural and social world, and made dynamic through a stress on convergence and unifying action. Teilhard's mysticism of action may simply be characterized as a mysticism of unification, a mysticism of transformation, and a mysticism of sanctification. It is a vision of wholeness closely linked to "a new definition of holiness"[41] which we are so much in need of; as he once wrote, a transformation "which will bring the universe from the material to the spiritual state."[42]

This understanding of a mysticism of action is set within an evolutionary dynamic of a world in transformation. Teilhard saw the world as "divine milieu," as the interpenetration of divine elements filled with a diaphanous luminosity capable to penetrate, transform, and transfigure everything. His mysticism of action is a mysticism of evolution, a new vision related to the development of a new world. Thus it grew out of a lifelong meditation on religious and scientific truths and is shaped by lifelong experience and action. His understanding of mysticism is linked to all that we are, all that we do, and all that we suffer, to the entire process of what he called in his book *The Divine*

Milieu "the divinisation of our activities" and "of our passivities." Thus his mysticism of action might also be described as a "mysticism of the divine milieu." For Teilhard human activity in all its forms was capable of divinization. As F.C. Happold (1971) pointed out in his comparative study and anthology, *Mysticism*, for Teilhard "union with God was not through withdrawal from the activity of the world but through a dedicated, integrated, and sublimated absorption in it." Happold called this a

> mysticism of action, action springing from the inspiration of a universe seen as moved and com-penetrated by God in the totality of its evolution . . . This is essentially a new type of mysticism, the result of a profound life-long, reconciling meditation on religious and scientific truth; and it is thus of immense relevance and significance for a scientific age such as ours.[43]

### 3. Mysticism and Contemporary Society

Too often, perhaps, mysticism is seen as primarily a historical phenomenon, yet we must ask, "What is its importance for society today?" This raises a host of further questions about the practice of mysticism in relationship to both personal spirituality and social action. Is mysticism primarily a personal-individual phenomenon which, through its influence on and interaction with others, has wide social implications?

Detailed discussions exist about possible criteria of distinction between mystical experience as distinct from numinous, ecstatic, or religious experience in general. These discussions may be of great interest to scholars on mysticism, but are perhaps less central to those concerned with the practice of mystical spirituality and its importance for society. Here the question, far less studied by scholars, is really *how to become a mystic.* Is this possible by self-effort alone, or to speak in religious terms, is divine grace required? What is the relationship between mystical consciousness and rational and ethical aspects of the human being? Do the ideals and practices of mystics have a conservative or a profoundly transforming and revolutionary effect on society at large?

Richard Kirby, in his work *The Mission of Mysticism* (1979),[44] has argued that mysticism has a mission to both the individual and the human race, while Adam Curle, in *Mystics and Militants* (1972),[45] relates the heightening of personal awareness to the growth of identity and transformative social action. In these, as in other cases, "mysticism" is broadly defined to mean a deep personal transformation linked to an expansion of consciousness and a one-centered, heightened awareness. The spiritual path pursued is not necessarily linked to one traditional religious "way," but makes use of methods, teachings, images, symbols, and insights from different religious and cultural traditions. The convergent tendencies are quite remarkable. However, this raises the further question of how far mysticism can be practiced and studied independently from religion. Psychotherapists like Arthur J. Deikman in *The Observing Self* (1982)[46] have argued that the mystical traditon has been concerned with the very problems that modern psychiatry has been unable to resolve; namely, the problems of meaning, the observing self, and the effect of motivation on consciousness. The insights of the mystical tradition can be used both for health and human development independently from religious traditions. Others draw selectively on the insights of different mystical traditions to highlight the parallels found in modern science, especially in the contemporary, "new physics" understanding of the nature of the cosmos, matter, and energy.

Thus we can note a number of divergent tendencies in the way different writers assess the value of mysticism for contemporary society. But whatever the overriding criteria by which comparisons and evaluations are made, there seems to be a general consensus pointing towards an increasing appreciation of the importance of mysticism and the example of past mystics, beyond the original context of their own religious tradition.

Mystics from all religious traditions, however diverse, seem to provide exemplars of a vision of faith, of a fundamental quality of life and being, which transcends and points beyond the doctrinal limitations of their respective religions. Wilfred Cantwell Smith in particular has emphasized the centrality of faith as the quality of persons and the source of meaning for whole cultures. He writes about this in relationship to contemporary Western society:

Something has gone profoundly wrong with Western humanism it would almost seem; maybe, if you didn't press the *religious*-faith emphasis, we could agree that our problem is perhaps our loss of faith — certainly if by faith you mean wholeness, integrity, loyalty, freedom, rapport. Above all, this is so if faith means meaningfulness: the ability to perceive life (one's own, one's neighbour's, the universe's) as "meaningful," to use that modern jargon. Those of us who perceive man's central problem as that of finding meaning, and even those of us who, more sceptically, hold that there is no meaning and that man's central problem accordingly is not to find it but to give it, to create meaning out of himself and herself — or to posit it, to generate it — both these groups see man's religious history as rather self-deluded yet significant movements constitutioning man's chief experiments in the past with the meaning problem.[47]

Religion as the deepest source of human energy providing meaning for both individual and social life is one of the central themes in Teilhard de Chardin's thought. According to him, religion has a central place in human evolution and the further development of human society at a global level, for he sees the entire world in the process of a spiritual transformation, linked to the rise of consciousness and that of the spirit. The "mystical sense" of human beings, defined as a fundamental quest for oneness and unification, is assuming planetary, global dimensions today as, in his view, the "mystical temperature" is rising to the same extent as human consciousness and self-reflection are growing.

It is not possible here to compare Teilhard de Chardin's vision of faith linked to a "new mysticism," a "mysticism of action and convergence," with the thought of other twentieth-century thinkers or spiritual teachers, such as Sri Aurobindo or Krishnamurti, for example. But they assign equal importance to a new spirituality and mysticism in shaping a new global vision and social ethic for the greater unification of humankind. To achieve the necessary transformation of contemporary society, it is not only helpful, but necessary to study and explore the rich diversity of all the resources the phenomenon of mysticism possesses, as Teilhard rightly emphasized. In this one can fully agree with him, even if one may disagree with the details of his own interpretation.

Part II

# Reflections on Interreligious Dialogue and Convergence

*6*

---

# Religion and the Future

TEILHARD DE CHARDIN'S THOUGHT AS CONTRIBUTION TO INTERRELIGIOUS DIALOGUE

Teilhard de Chardin often reflected on the importance of religion for the evolution of the future. How far can religion bring about a greater social integration of humankind? How far can it channel aspirations towards a higher future and furnish a focal center of attraction for humanity's further self-evolution?

Although religion might have a significant role to play in achieving greater social coherence, Teilhard's approach to religion is not primarily functional, exclusively interested in the role of religion in society, which might be analyzed in a detached manner. On the contrary, he looks at religion first and foremost as a committed believer who emphasizes the active quality of faith as an animating and spiritualizing force in human life. Lived *engagement* was an essential ingredient of his own experience and thought. This led him not to a dogmatic defense of the doctrinal statements of religion, but rather to a philosophical reflection on the dynamic elements of openness and growth that ought to be part of genuine religiousness. These qualities are of central importance for the building up of the kind of future envisaged by Teilhard's evolutionary perspective. Consequently, he is less concerned with examining religion as a phenomenon of the past than he is with studying religion as an agent of change for the future. His chief interests, therefore, revolve around the role of religion for the future, as well as the future of religion.

In discussing Teilhard's thought on religion, one has to keep in mind that it stems from several basic sources. His interpretation of the scientific data of evolution from the depths of geological time to the present led him to expect a higher future, where the morphological evolution of the human being would find its culmination in a further social evolution, leading ultimately to a convergence of humankind. His deep personal commitment to the Christian faith made him see Christ as universal redeemer who is closely related to a "cosmic emergence of the Spirit." He interpreted the data of evolution in the light of revelation and together they provided the basis for his great eschatological hope.[1] In addition, he was also much influenced by his lifelong experience of the scientific and religious milieux of Europe, America, and the Far East. The open encounter of different believers and unbelievers, whom he had frequent occasion to meet, shaped in him certain views regarding the necessary reorientation of religion so that it can meet the future spiritual needs of humankind.

The combination of these personal-experiential and scientific-interpretative dimensions supplied Teilhard the criteria by which he evaluated the living religions. Their respective value depends on the contribution which the existing religions can make towards nourishing our belief in and our energy for building up the future. Their relative strength is related to the extent to which they can bring about a deeper unity of humankind by integrating all people "not only with their ground which is God but also with each other and with all things through God."[2] Teilhard's entire work is permeated by this approach and one can find frequent references to religion in many of his essays. In fact, all his writings can be interpreted from a religious point of view.[3] His views on religion have found explicit expression in several important essays. The present chapter is particularly based on those found in the two volumes *The Future of Man* and *Science and Christ*.[4]

Teilhard's major ideas on religion can be discussed under the following headings:

1. The historical multiplicity of human religious experience.

2. The present religious situation of humankind.

3. The necessary integration of two types of faith.

4. The role of religion in shaping the future.

### 1. The Historical Multiplicity of Human Religious Experience

Teilhard's close scientific study of the early origins of humankind as a biological species led him to consider the importance of the rich variety of human civilizations, including their respective religions. Historically speaking, human civilizations grew "in patches." Separated in space and time, they were often completely isolated from each other or occasionally interdependent. The different peoples and cultures of the globe have known an independent upsurge and growth of the religious spirit, a deep questioning of the meaning of human life in the universe, and a longing for union with an Ultimate Reality.

The age of civilizations is now definitely coming to an end. After the initial expansion all over the globe through prehistoric and all of historical time, humankind has now entered a new phase of "compression" where further geographical expansion is near its limits. The increasing density of populations and the acute limitations of global resources compel people to begin to unite. The mere physical nearness of people (illustrated at its best in the steadily growing urbanization all over the world) brings with it also a greater interaction, interconnection, and interdependence. This trend is further strengthened through modern means of transport and communications and has been exponentially increased through the revolution in electronics. Gradually, the present developments will lead to the evolution of one single organism and civilization, characterized by one "noosphere" or single field of human thought.

In the same way, a further evolution of the great religions can be foreseen as none of the living religious traditions can any longer continue to exist in complete isolation among people otherwise more and more interconnected. The forces of "compression," at present working everywhere towards greater unification, cannot bypass the religious sphere. Thus interreligious dialogue and mutual enrichment of the different religious traditions will have to come of necessity.

Teilhard was fully conscious of the rich and often confusing variety of religious phenomena in human history. Yet it is neither the seemingly irreducible diversity of the human element in religion nor the transcendent unity of the Divine which is his overriding concern. His emphasis lies with the dynamic potential that religion can have in harnessing together the deepest spiritual energies so that these may become the main driving force towards the evolution of a higher future. For him, religion of all times and kinds is related to the human being's basic need of the Absolute; it gives us "a dominating principle or order and an axis of movement... something of supreme value, to create, to hold in awe, or to love."[5] It is the biological function of religion to give a form to the spiritual energies released in the cosmos with the development of the human species. Because of the advent of *noogenesis*—the thrust forward of life towards consciousness and self-reflective thought—an "ocean of free energy"[6] is created, an energy as real and as cosmic as the energy in matter. With the steadily progressing self-evolution of the human being, religion, too, must grow and redefine itself.

There are many contemporary factors that point towards a growing unity of human consciousness. According to Teilhard, there is also a growing awareness of both the unity of religions and the importance of mysticism for religion. He wrote:

> Present-day Mankind, as it becomes increasingly aware of its unity—not only past unity in the blood, but future unity in progress—is experiencing a vital need to close in upon itself. A tendency towards unification is everywhere manifest, and especially in the different branches of religion. We are looking for something that will draw us together, below or above the level of that which divides.[7]

However, before Teilhard's views on the unifying forces in religion can be fully discussed, let us look at his analysis of the present religious situation of humankind.

## 2. *The Present Religious Situation of Humankind*

Teilhard repeatedly pointed out both our immense power to utilize and manipulate the resources of the world and those within ourselves, and the increasing ambiguity of this situation. The evolution of the past has reached its summit in human self-reflection, but it does not come to a standstill there. A future evolution is both necessary and unavoidable. Yet the determination of its course will depend on the planned use of our collective power of invention and reflection. We hold, so to speak, all the future in our own hands; it is our responsibility to decide which further direction the evolution of humankind will take. Thus the problem of *right human action* and the *ultimate quality of human thought and life* are of primary importance:

> . . . we have the simultaneous growth in our minds of two essentially modern concepts, those of collectivity and of an organic future: a double development precisely engendering the deep-rooted change of heart that was required to bring about the direct transformation of a childlike and instinctive faith in Man into its rational, adult state of constructive, militant faith in Mankind! A spiritual crisis was inevitable; it has not been slow in coming. But let us look with open minds at the new world being born around us . . . If we have any power of vision we are bound to recognize that the ills which so afflict us are above all growing-pains. What looks like no more than a hunger for material well-being is in reality a hunger for higher being: it is the spirit of Mankind suddenly alive with the sense of all that remains to be done if it is to achieve the fulfillment of its powers and possibilities.[8]

The contemporary turmoil, manifest in so many events, bears all the signs of a spiritual crisis. The reason for this is that humanity, at the very peak of its power, "has not defined its spiritual pole. It lacks religion."[9] But the kind of religion it lacks cannot be found in the religious traditions of the past which, originally, are linked to static categories. What is needed is a new religion full of "dynamics" and "conquests," a religion that can utilize all the "free energy" of the earth to build humankind into greater unity.

The contemporary spiritual crisis is due to the fact that our vision of the world has been profoundly modified over a few generations through the discovery of the physical evolution and then, the realization of a psychic evolution in the universe. The combined influence of the findings of science and history, and the discovery of our social dimension have led to an experience of duration and collectivity on a scale unknown before. Thus human consciousness finds itself on the threshold of a new age which requires entirely new dimensions and values.

The historical roots of this transformation of our self-understanding have often been analyzed by Teilhard and are summarized in the following passage:

> To our clearer vision the universe is no longer a State but a Process. The cosmos has become a Cosmogenesis. And it may be said without exaggeration that, directly or indirectly, all the intellectual crises through which civilisation has passed in the last four centuries arise out of the successive stages whereby a static *Weltanschauung* has been and is being transformed, in our minds and hearts, into a *Weltanschauung* of movement. In the early stage, that of Galileo, it may have seemed that the stars alone were affected. But the Darwinian stage showed that the cosmic process extends from sidereal space to life on earth; with the result that, in the present phase, Man finds himself overtaken and borne on the whirlwind which his own silence has discovered and, as it were, unloosed . . . This is a major event which must lead, as we shall see, to the profound modification of the whole structure not only of our Thought but of our Beliefs.[10]

The deepest beliefs of human beings, that is, their search and experience of the Absolute and the very language in which these are articulated, must find new forms of expression. Anyone who is aware of contemporary spiritual needs must realize the insufficiency of historical answers to completely new questions, the inadequacy of past formulations for present lives.

Today humanity is restless, doubtful, relentlessly questioning and experimenting. We seem to undergo an almost permanent crisis of identity and approach traditional beliefs with ever-growing scepticism. The repercussions of these doubts can be felt among all religions, as none of them has been able to provide an adequate answer for our contemporary spiritual problems:

. . .for some obscure reason something has gone wrong between Man and God *as in these days He is represented to Man.* Man would seem to have no clear picture of the God he longs to worship. Hence (despite certain positive indications of re-birth which are, however, still largely obscured) the impression one gains from everything taking place around us is of an irresistible growth of atheism — or more exactly, a mounting and irresistible de-Christianisation.

Elsewhere he writes, "The human world of today has not grown cold, but it is ardently searching for a God proportionate to the newly discovered immensities of a Universe whose aspect exceeds the present compass of our power of worship."[11]

Given the vast dimensions of the universe, many contemporaries find it impossible to accept certain traditional representations of God or certain forms of adoration. Teilhard thought this was so because our image of God is often "not worthy of the universe we know."[12] People today are essentially not "a-religious" but against the past narrowness of particular religions against which they revolt. There is a wide attempt which finds expression in such diverse contemporary phenomena as philosophical and literary atheism, dialectic Marxism, the slogans of a new humanism, the reinterpretations of Christian theology proposed by Bultmann, Tillich, and other theologians, the suggestion of a "religionless Christianity" made by Bonhoeffer, and the debate over a "God-is-dead" theology in the West.

Teilhard did not judge modern atheism negatively but understood it as the expression of an intrinsic malaise and also as a pointer towards the development of new forms of religiousness:

A certain pessimism around us repeats that our world is foundering into atheism. Instead, should one not rather say that what it is suffering from is an *unsatisfied theism?* — You say, men do not want God any longer. Are you really sure that they do not simply reject the image of a God which has become too small to nourish in us that interest to go on living and to live on a higher plane to which, in the end, one must relate the need for adoration?[13]

At present people's faith seems to be primarily directed towards this world, and yet the very ardor of this faith is linked to something more:

...neo-human faith in the World, to the extent that it is truly a Faith (that is to say, entailing sacrifice and the final abandonment of self for something greater) necessarily implies an element of worship, the acceptance of something *divine.* Every conversation I have ever had with communist intellectuals has left me with a decided impression that Marxist atheism is not absolute, but that it simply rejects an "extrinsical" God, a *deus ex machina* whose existence can only undermine the dignity of the Universe and weaken the springs of human endeavor—a "pseudo-God," in short, whom no one in these days any longer wants...[14]

In some notes on "Modern Unbelief," written in 1933, Teilhard tried to analyze both the cause of and the remedy for contemporary atheism.[15] Speaking from his experience as a Christian, he sees the ultimate cause for people's abandonment of the Christian faith in the fact that traditional Christianity is too much at variance with "the natural religious current" of contemporary humanity. This religious current has the universe as its object of adoration and thus appears to be in opposition to the worship of the traditional Christian God.

Teilhard discussed characteristics of these two apparently opposed beliefs in detail. The world, immersed in the steadily rising movement of becoming and growth, attracts our natural powers of adoration. This new "religion of the world" has made many converts among contemporaries. Its positive strength consists in the predominance given to the whole over any of its parts, the passionate faith in the value and possibilities of human effort, and the vivid perception of the sacred character of all research. In comparison, Christianity seems to foster disdain and fear of progress and discovery. Consequently, the highest and most strongly felt aspirations of our contemporaries seem neither nourished nor consecrated by the Christian faith. The "revealed God" appears at present to be overshadowed by a "world-God." Yet it must be mentioned that contemporary religious aspirations, despite their strong this-worldly orientation, lack a clear outline and shape. They are often vague, in search of something more definite and stable. Many of the present gropings reflect humanity's effort "to find its soul," to envisage a center or pole towards which it can aspire and direct its growth.

Teilhard thought that there might be a remedy to this situation by trying to show that the deepest natural aspirations of humankind can be affirmed and centered in a wider conception of the Christian faith, a faith that would truly incorporate the values of the world and animate human beings in their search for the future. Thus the faith in the "revealed God" and the "world-God" are not really opposed but only two aspects of what is fundamentally a search for the same reality. The synthesis of these two aspects has not been found yet; it is still a task to be achieved. It was one of Teilhard's major preoccupations to show that these two types of faith can and have to be assimilated into one.

### 3. The Necessary Integration of Two Types of Faith

The change in human self-understanding as a being-in-history-and-cosmos must lead to a change in the understanding of God: theology has to be related to anthropology. All traditional religions originated in historically and geographically limited cultures, none of which possessed an awareness of the collective unity and common destiny of humankind equal to the one we experience today. It is all the more surprising, therefore, that the great religions have proclaimed a message of universal love and salvation. This message, however, is mostly addressed to the individual and less to collective humanity. It is generally the individual who is called to conversion, personal holiness, and fulfillment in a Beyond.

For Teilhard, this traditional perspective of "a religion of individuals and of heaven" is insufficient; people are looking for a "religion of mankind and of the earth"[16] which gives meaning to human achievements, a place to cosmic and human evolution in the ultimate scheme of things, and a deep sense of commitment to the development of this earth to its utmost limits:

> The true struggle we are witnessing is not between believers and unbelievers, but between two sorts of believers. Two ideals, two conceptions of the Divine, are confronting one another... A religion of the earth is being mobilised against the religion of heaven. That is the basic situation, in all its gravity but also in the hopes it contains.[17]

Fundamentally, humankind is divided between those who will "stake their soul on a future greater than themselves and those who, through inertia, selfishness, or because they have lost heart, have no wish to press on."[18] Having met believers and unbelievers in a genuine spirit of openness, Teilhard tried to find a basis for a possible "common human creed."[19] The precise point of divergence among the different religious and neo-humanist faiths is the value which they attach to God *or* the world, to the attainment of an utterly transcendent or an entirely immanent future. This difference cuts across all traditional religions and beliefs. Both the faith in God and the faith in this world are a source of magnificent spiritual energy in human beings. But both elans ultimately converge if one admits the reality of a *noogenesis*, of a cosmic emergence of the Spirit. Thus

> the believer in this World will find himself compelled to allow increasing room, in his vision of the future, for the values of personalisation and transcendency... On the other hand, the believer in Heaven, accepting this same reality of a cosmic genesis of the Spirit, must perceive that the mystical evolution of which he dreams presupposes and consecrates all the tangible realities and all the arduous conditions of human progress... [20]

The necessary synthesis between the two types of faith — faith in the world and faith in God — cannot be found otherwise than in individual human beings who achieve it as a lived reality. It is not a synthesis that scholars can work out on the abstract level of learning, but an integration which is realized on the concrete level of existence. We need people "who will be passionately and *simultaneously* animated in both types of faith and so effect in themselves, *in one heart*, the junction of two mystical forces... men who are all the more convinced of the sacred value of human effort in that they are primarily interested in God."[21]

Teilhard criticized the dominantly "other-worldly" orientation of traditional religions. He saw something ultrahuman being born in the future through the continued shaping of the human being whose further self-evolution was bound to have a deep effect on religious faith:

For the spiritually minded, whether in the East or the West, one point has hitherto not been in doubt: that Man could only attain to a fuller life by rising "vertically" above the material zones of the world. Now we see the possibility of an entirely different line of progress. The Higher Life, the Union, the long-dreamed-of consummation that has hitherto been sought *Above*, in the direction of some kind of transcendency: should we not rather look for it *Ahead*, in the prolongation of the inherent forces of evolution? Above or ahead—or both? [22]

The vertical dimension of seeking "God on high," of searching for a God entirely transcendent to this world, has to be integrated with a horizontal dimension of "God ahead," the "God within," whose operative power is gradually being revealed in the unfolding of the evolutionary process itself. This may be only another way of expressing the traditional idea of an immanent and transcendent Absolute, but if one considers the basic mutation which has taken place in post-Darwinian, post-Marxian and post-Freudian consciousness, then the understanding of divine immanence in the cosmic and historical processes of the world must also assume new dimensions.

The ultimate source of the modern religious crisis consists, according to Teilhard, in an acute conflict between upward and forward, in the confrontation of two types of faith, one of which believes in "the transcendent action of a personal God" and the other in the "innate perfectibility of a World in progress."[23] It is only through the integration of both types of faith that human beings can develop a really evolutionary élan and a "taste for life." Such an integrated faith alone can inspire the radiant spirit of love—the only kind of spiritual energy capable of causing the formidable human organism to develop to its maximum capacity without the danger of destruction from either egotism or totalitarianism.

The new being needed by humankind for its further evolution—the "*homo progressivus*." as Teilhard sometimes says— cannot evade the ambiguity of the contemporary situation characterized by "the grand option"[24] between the rejection of this world or its perfection but, religiously speaking, the human being is also faced with the immense temptation of refusing God:

"Given the power he possesses, why should Man look for a God outside himself? Man, self-sufficient and wholly autonomous, sole master and disposer of his destiny and the world's — is not this an even nobler concept?" This is the modern version of "the heroic temptation of all time, that of the Titans, or Prometheus, of Babel and of Faust; that of Christ on the mountain; a temptation as old as the Earth itself."[25] It is the ultimate *hybris* of human beings who can only see themselves and their own works, which become the center of their worship.

Teilhard deeply believed, however, that "faith in Man does not exclude but must on the contrary include the worship of Another — One who is higher than Man." Correctly interpreted, "Faith in Man can and indeed must cast us at the feet and into the arms of One who is greater than ourselves."[26] For him, the spirit of sacrifice and union is centered on the expectation of a future apotheosis. His wide vision perceived "the rise on our inward horizon of a cosmic spiritual center, a supreme pole of consciousness, upon which all the separate consciousnesses of the world may converge and within which they may love one another: *the rise of a God.*"[27]

Used to the vast magnitudes of the geological time-scale, Teilhard did not conceive of the future as the immediate morrow, but as prolonging itself far ahead into time. At present and perhaps for a long time to come, the "Faustian spirit" might oppose the "Christian spirit" of union between the faith in humanity and in God. The "Faustian spirit" believes that humankind possesses an inherent ability to further perfect itself through its own powers, while the "Christian spirit" tends towards "the union with a God who supports and draws us to him through all the forces of a world in evolution."[28]

This opposition is the old conflict between religion and science in a new form. When writing on this in 1946, Teilhard thought that, on the whole, pure scientists still tended more toward the "Faustian spirit" of exclusive self-reliance than towards the spirit of union. This is perhaps no longer true to the same extent today. In any case, it was Teilhard's firm conviction that ultimately only the spirit of union could supply the new values and animating love necessary for the advance of humankind towards a new order. Humanity needs a divine guarantee that the fruits of its labors are not lost and its achievements not in vain. Such a guarantee can only be supplied by "an objective that is capable, *because its nature is super-personal,* of releasing deep in our souls the forces of love, beside which other forms of spiritual energy fade into insignificance and are nothing."[29]

For Teilhard, higher socialization and higher personalization are correlated; one cannot be achieved without the other. The higher development of humankind is seen to find its ultimate focus in a superpersonal center which he calls the pole Omega. The evolutionary process, steadily rising to higher and higher consciousness, must ultimately converge at this supreme point, which animates and attracts the forces of evolution throughout the cosmos and humankind. This pole Omega is the indwelling spirit, the "spiritual face" of the world, and at the same time, the final focus of convergence of human and divine:

> . . . the Universe is illumined from within: that is to say, it shows itself to be capable of fulfilling the highest of our mystical aspirations. By virtue of the convergence of the cosmic lines . . . we must surmise the existence of a higher centre of consciousness ahead of us, at the apogee of Evolution. But if we seek to determine the position and analyse the properties of this Supreme Centre it soon becomes clear that we must look far beyond and far above any mere aggregation of perfected Mankind. If it is to be capable of joining together in itself the prolonged fibres of the world, the apex of the cone within which we move can be conceived only as something that is ultra-conscious, ultra-personalised, ultra-present.[30]

Teilhard's deep faith in the person of Christ made him identify this supreme center of evolution with the final, full revelation of God in Christ. In fact, it was his Christian faith which perhaps first suggested the idea of the pole Omega as the summit of convergence for the forces of evolution: "Christ coincides . . . with what I have called . . . Omega Point."[31] "The revealed Christ is nothing else but Omega . . . '*Omnia in omnibus Christus*'. . . That is the very definition of Omega!"[32]

Generally writing for a wider public than the Christian, Teilhard often speaks of the pole Omega without direct reference to Christ. He was very fond of using two images to illustrate the nature of this convergence: As the upward layers of a cone converge at their summit, so humanity will converge at the pole Omega. This image implies steady growth and a tendency towards greater unification inherent *within* humankind itself. The other image is that of the "human tide" which is steadily rising towards Omega. This implicitly refers to the strong attractive forces which the pole Omega exercises on humanity from *without*, similar to the tide of water, carried upwards not through itself but through outside forces acting upon it.

The true religion of progress, the religion of evolution which Teilhard envisages, is an integration of both our faith in the development and perfectibility of this world and the faith in God as the activating force and focus of attraction which makes this development fundamentally possible. It is not a mere compromise between the God of old and the movements of the contemporary world, but a reorientation of faith altogether:

> The sense of the earth opening and exploding upwards into God; and the sense of God taking root and finding nourishment downwards into Earth. A personal, transcendent God and an evolving Universe no longer forming two hostile centres of attraction, but entering into hierarchic conjunction to raise the human mass on a single tide. Not only does the idea of a possible raising of our consciousness to a state of super-consciousness show itself daily, in the light of scientific experience, to be better founded . . . but furthermore this idea . . . appears to be the only one capable of paving the way for the great event we look for — the manifestation of a unified impulse of worship in which will be joined and mutually exalted both a passionate desire to conquer the World and a passionate longing to be united with God: the vital act, specifically new, corresponding to a new age in the history of the Earth.[33]

Teilhard repeatedly affirmed his faith in the progress of humankind to an extent which we, in a more sceptical age disillusioned with overly fast change, find difficult to share. But he was all too aware that the next forward step in human collective development could only be taken if humanity found a "new soul" to bring a new world into being. For this to happen, religion is indispensable.

## 4. The Role of Religion in Shaping the Future

In the immense task of achieving a future breakthrough for humankind, religions have an "evolutionary role"[34] to play by animating and harnessing together the deepest spiritual energies of human beings. The "progressive humanisation of humanity" which Teilhard envisages depends ultimately on the "mystic current" of humankind which nourishes our "need to be," our "taste for life," and the "ardent desire to grow." It has been said that the mystics of all traditions have been the ones most successful in each community in understanding people of divergent faiths. Yet, according to Teilhard, the upward or inward orientation of traditional mysticism needs to be combined with a forward or outward direction which, instead of rejecting and annihilating human endeavor, brings it to its fullest achievement.

Teilhard speaks of a selection and general convergence of the different religious traditions according to their capacity to animate and nourish the evolutionary drive in human beings. As is the case with other Teilhardian concepts, the term *convergence* in this context is rather vague. It is meant to suggest and explore the general direction of a development rather than to circumscribe one definite event. It must also be pointed out that despite the occasional similarity of his evolutionary terms to those of an exclusive humanism, Teilhard does not advocate a new religion of humanity or a syncretistic substitute for the old religions. The uniting force between the different religions, the axis on which their convergence or one might suggest instead, their dialogue and encounter, can begin, is their respective faith in the human being. But this faith is intrinsically linked to an ultimate vision of God or of an Ultimate, fragments of which are found in every religion. But even more precious than these fragments of vision are "the experiences of contact with a supreme Ineffable"[35] which the different religious traditions preserve and transmit.

Inspired by the perspective of ultimate convergence, Teilhard found sufficient grounds for criticizing both Western and Eastern religions. He equally deplored the pessimism about human progress found among many Christians and the world-denying attitude of Eastern religions, for which the spiritual ascent of human beings often seems to depend on a negation of the illusory "phenomena" of the world. Pessimistic Christians might almost indiscriminately condemn anything new "without seeing among the blemishes and evils the hallowed efforts of something that is being born."[36] Although contemporary Christianity still lacks sincerity in its attitude towards this-worldly values and needs to be rethought "*with all that is human in us,*"[37] Teilhard was convinced that, ultimately, the animating and "amorizing" forces which humankind needs can only come from the universal and cosmic Christ, both divine and human. Thus Christianity supplies the central axis for the evolution of religion because of its intrinsic capacity for hope and optimism. It is the true religion of progress, the "very religion of evolution."[38]

The decisive test for evaluating the traditional religions is the strength of their capacity to lead humankind to closer unity and finally to convergence. "The biological function of religion is to give a form to the free psychic energy of the world. And the only form which the development of mankind can accept, is that of a process of construction and conquest that leads up to some supreme unification of the universe."[39] This is, in fact, the determining factor by which the value of the various religious traditions must be judged.

Looking at Teilhard's thought from a wider perspective, one can see that he stressed the growing importance of mysticism and interreligious dialogue to bring about a greater coming together of humankind. All the traditional religions have developed certain "definite axes of justice and holiness"[40] and produced admirable and progressive codes of perfection. Yet these were developed and are generally maintained outside the perspectives of a universe in evolution. Contemporary people need a truly incarnational spirituality which offers a divine center that emerges out of the cosmos and is at the same time immersed in it. Only such a spirituality can be a true religion of progress. For Teilhard this animating center of spiritual energy is the point Omega, the goal of human evolution. In his view:

> The universe cannot *be thought of as fully meeting the requirements, both extrinsic and intrinsic of anthropogenesis* unless it takes on the form of a convergent psychic milieu. It must necessarily reach its

fulfillment, ahead of us, in some pole of super-consciousness in which all the personalised grains of consciousness survive and "super-live." It culminates in an *Omega Point.* Christ coincides. . . with what I earlier called Omega Point. In virtue of his position as the Omega of the world, Christ. . . represents the focus point towards which and in which all things *converge*. . . he appears as a Person with whom all reality. . . effects an approach and a contact in the only direction that is possible: *the line in which their centre lies*. . . . every operation, once it is directed towards him, assumes. . . the psychical character of a centre-to-centre relationship. . . of an act of love.[41]

Animated by this perspective of seeing all human achievements as ultimately centered in the Divine, Teilhard believed that religion still had an important role in society. The religion of the future is a religion that incorporates and saves the new religious needs of people today. At the same time, it is a religion sustained and guided by the tradition of the great mystics so that, through contemplation and prayer, we may enter directly "into receptive communication with the very source of all inner effort."[42]

R.C. Zaehner has remarked that Teilhard's position represents an essentially Christian mysticism—a mysticism of affirmation and solidarity as against a mysticism of negation and isolation.[43] It would perhaps be more apt to interpret Teilhard's all-embracing vision from a wider perspective as related to an extrovertive or outward-looking rather than an introvertive or inward-looking type of mystical experience.[44]

Leaving particular distinctions aside and following Teilhard's universalistic perspective, none of the religions in the present is fully adequate for our development towards a higher future. The religious consciousness of people everywhere needs a dynamic reorientation, and to achieve this, the dialogue between Eastern and Western religious traditions is both a necessity and an important step in the future evolution of humankind.

Teilhard does not advocate a mere comparison of religious doctrines and rituals. His vision of the evolutionary role of religion asks for a genuine dialogue between the existing religions, a dialogue that involves existential participation, leading to the mutual enrichment of the various religious traditions. The worldwide encounter of these traditions and the integration of their most valuable insights is, in the words of Raimundo Panikkar, itself "a religious event." This new event is beginning to take shape now and Teilhard predicted of it:

> . . . one might say that a hitherto unknown form of religion—one that no one could as yet have imagined or described for lack of a universe large enough and organic enough to contain it—is burgeoning in the heart of modern man, from a seed sown by the idea of evolution. God is no longer sought in an identification with things that annihilates personality, nor from an escape that dehumanises man. God is attained (and this is infinitely more energizing and brings infinitely truer communion) by entry into the total sphere that embraces all things—a centre that is itelf in formation. Far from being shaken in my faith by such a revolution, it is with irrepressible hope that I welcome the rise of this new mysticism and anticipate its equally inevitable triumph.[45]

Teilhard's vision of the unique and decisive role of religion for humanity's evolution towards a higher future can be inspiring and helpful in creating the right spirit for interreligious dialogue. Although Teilhard himself may never have used the term *interreligious dialogue*, his life and work were imbued with its spirit. Speaking to our contemporaries who, with their scientific, evolutionary, and global outlook, are growing more and more into citizens of the world, Teilhard emphasized the need for integrating humankind's total religious experience into a new spirituality for a new world being born. The beginning of this integration is found in encounter and dialogue.

Interreligious dialogue as an existential encounter occurring in the present must of necessity be concerned with the future. Such a concern relates to the contribution of religion to the future of humankind as well as the future of religion. It is on both these questions that Teilhard de Chardin has something of special value to say. Yet his reflections on the future must be related to a still larger horizon, for the range of his ideas can only be fully understood if one takes into account further perspectives on the convergence of religions, the contribution of world faiths, and the development of a new mysticism of action centered on the phenomenon of love, as will be seen in the following chapters.

# Exploring Convergence: The Contribution of World Faiths

"Exploring Convergence" seems a particularly suitable theme in honor of Sir Francis Younghusband,[1] for the idea of a convergence is associated with the coming or drawing together at a summit, with a search for a center or peak not yet reached, a unity yet to be born, but not yet existent. It is also one of the central themes of Teilhard de Chardin's thought, as will become clear later. Teilhard de Chardin once referred to the World Congress of Faiths as a "summit movement," thereby stressing its importance in finding unity among the world religions, as well as the need to find a focal point, a summit for diverse religious aspirations.

Sir Francis Younghusband, the founder of the World Congress of Faiths, underwent a profound religious experience on a mountainside in Tibet. He had a transforming vision from a summit which made him see everything anew. Many religious seers and people from different faiths have undergone similar experiences, both in the past and in the present, and they have commented on the transforming power such a peak experience can exercise and the change of perspective it can introduce into one's life. Believers of all traditions bear testimony to the fact that faith at its deepest, at an existential level of commitment, transforms one's vision of the world and offers, in the word of a contemporary, a wonderfully novel and clear view as from the peak of a mountain range. Let us consider how the world faiths relate to convergence by asking three questions: 1) What does convergence imply, and does it exist in the contemporary world? 2) If a movement of convergence exists, how does it affect the world religions? 3) What contribution can the world faiths make towards the convergence of humankind?

### 1. What Does Convergence Imply?

We shall begin with the question, "What is meant by convergence?" "To converge" initially means to draw or come together; at the simplest level it is said of lines which tend to meet at one point. Yet when one speaks of the possible convergence of humankind, or the convergence of religions, one is not thinking of something linear and straightforward like a geometrical projection. Rather, convergence is to be thought of as a multidimensional, complex process operating at many different levels. It is not unity in the sense of uniformity, but it implies a complex network of relationships among different parts. Convergence in this sense means the search for, or the movement towards, a common meeting point through which we can interrelate and create a unity that transcends our diverse particularities. The idea of convergence presents a vision of unity and universality which, at present, remains largely an ideal rather than being a fact. Some shun the very concept of convergence as having idealist overtones, for a movement of convergence can easily be misconstrued as meaning a simple blending or syncretistic fusion wherein all separate distinctions are blurred and all identities lost. However, I am not using the word in this syncretistic sense.

If we remain at the factual rather than the ideal level, one might say that there seems to be little convergence in the world today. On closer inspection, however, one can discern two opposite movements; in fact, one can talk about a striking paradox in contemporary civilization: To many, if not to most of us, the world seems deeply torn apart, full of dissension, war, injustice, and bloodshed—in short, marked by divergence and disunity. And yet, seen from another perspective, there are also many movements at work towards greater economic, political, and cultural unity which aim at the closer coming together and convergence of humankind. Contemporary civilization is marked by the simultaneous existence of, on one hand, a drive towards greater unification and, on the other, a constantly growing diversification. As much emphasis is placed on individuality and particularity as on the need for greater social integration and universality.

The past has no parallels to the way contemporary civilization is coming to be centered upon the consciousness of humankind as ultimately one community. Movements towards greater unification are at work in many fields of human endeavor, including the area of world religions. Never before in human history have so many believed in the oneness of humankind, a oneness pertaining to people's common origin, shared development, and a unity of purpose. This oneness is not actually given; it is not real yet, but it exists as an ideal, a deeply felt need and a dream which many wish to come true.

Yet at the moment what little unity has been achieved has largely come about through external forces, through pressures and necessity. It is a mechanistic rather than an organic unity. However, true unity and coherence can only be brought about by mutual acceptance and love. At the moment, we are merely at a stage of *confluence*, an external gathering which still lacks direction and a common goal. True *convergence*, however, implies an overall direction and orientation; it includes the vision of a common meeting point or summit where different currents can converge. The process of convergence thus means unification through and beyond differentiation.

Many signs in the contemporary world point to a change of age and direction. There is a growing consciousness of a "converging world," of a movement towards a real and realizable unity. But will the dream come true? Will there ultimately be greater unity and integration, or will humankind develop towards more irreconcilable states of division? Both possibilities are open at present; which road we choose will depend on us. The future of humankind, whether united or divided, will be our responsibility and our creation. The idea of convergence presents a goal of unity, for it will not come about automatically. Convergence is by no means an inevitable process but an ideal to be chosen—or to be rejected as the case may be. Convergence will come about if we foster its development. At the moment, we can already discern a certain amount of cultural convergence in the areas of science and technology and the global network of communications. Let us ask what effect such developments have on the situation of the world religions and then examine the idea of a possible convergence of religions.

## 2. How Does Convergence Affect World Religions?

The existing process of cultural convergence has revolutionary implications for the different world religions. Will they cease to exist, will they remain separate in a convergent culture, or will they themselves converge? In many ways, religions have become a cultural "remnant" in modern society; they no longer mold the patterns of social life or shape major social institutions in the way they did in the past. From being a Western development first, secularization is now increasingly becoming a global phenomenon; it has been defined as a process whereby religion is losing its social significance. But does this imply that religion is a dying phenomenon, as one sociologist put it recently? Sufficient counter-evidence seems to exist in contemporary life and literature to show that questions of ultimate meaning are more important than ever for the individual, and for society, too. Can the great religions provide some of the answers?

Human thought has greatly increased its capacity for self-reflective examination and projection. Humanity's range of choice has grown so vast that the question of the decisive values on which to base our actions is all the more crucial. How do the world religions relate to this revolution in human consciousness? Can they give meaning to the "change of epoch" we are experiencing? Can they respond creatively to the historically new situation of cultural convergence? Perhaps not many religious leaders in the contemporary world are fully aware of the importance of these questions. Unfortunately they are often more concerned with the preservation of past traditions than with an innovative and creative approach to the religious situation of people today.

In the past, religious traditions developed for the most part independently of each other in separate cultural and historical contexts. When religions did come into contact with each other, it was usually in a situation of either contrast or exclusive opposition where one attempted to either dominate, supplant, or conquer the other. In a politically postcolonial world all societies are economically, technically, and scientifically more closely brought together; cooperation has to develop on the basis of egalitarian partnership. This new situation applies also to the encounter of religions. We have to seek what has been called a unitive interpretation of religion whereby the different religious traditions understand and refer to each other in a mutually meaningful way. With the increasing expansion of our boundaries of knowledge, we are also gaining a growing acquaintance of each other's religious heritage. This may be seen as a merely quantitative development, but one should not underestimate the possible qualitative effect of this knowledge *about* world religions on the very nature of religious awareness in the modern world. Taking full cognizance of the religious experience of humankind may lead to what has been characterized as a "global religious consciousness." It may bring about a true mutation in religious awareness, a new awakening to what is most central to all faith and genuine spirituality, on a scale unknown in the past.

However, this change in religious awareness, of which we can discern many signs today, is mainly taking place outside the traditional boundaries of religious institutions, and it is largely beyond institutional control. It represents a genuinely open religious quest cutting across all denominations and religious differences. The sincerity and authenticity of the religious search of many of our contemporaries, particularly the young, cannot be questioned but must be respected and admired.

Teilhard de Chardin first spoke of convergence almost fifty years ago. His vision of the interrelatedness of all people and all beliefs was very much born out of lived experience. Travels in Europe, the Americas, Africa, and Asia, particularly in China, brought home to him the immensity of the earth and its peoples.

He deeply felt the intense desire and mounting movement as well as the urgent need for a closer coming together of humankind, however little articulated and centered such a movement at present may be. His thoughts also increasingly focused on the question of humanity's responsibility for shaping its own future. This includes the important question of the role of religion and its value for contemporary society.

Although Teilhard de Chardin possessed no particular competence in the history of religions and expressed certain views which are too ethnocentric and narrow from a contemporary perspective, he was looking at the world's religions with an unusual openness and a vision of universality which even today only a few would seem to possess. Throughout his life, he fought religious and scientific orthodoxies alike. He looked for a mutual enrichment and complementarity between East and West at the deepest level, the spiritual level. A dehumanizing spirituality was denounced wherever he found it—and examples could be cited from all religions. Teilhard wished to uncover and develop the truly dynamic and world-transforming elements within the "active currents of faiths" or what are usually called the "living religions." Few modern writers have felt so strongly and expressed so insistently the need for a new kind of spirituality in a new kind of world.

The structure of human thought and the nature of human society have changed so radically that many people are experiencing a profound crisis of meaning and identity which, in turn, has led to a crisis of the religions themselves. At present all religions are in a situation of trial, of a deep resifting and rethinking. At the very peak of its power, humanity has not yet found a spiritual pole: it lacks religion. To attract and channel the deepest human aspirations of the present, religions need to be dynamic, able to inspire and animate action and zest for life. They must do more than help the individual; they must address humanity at large.

In the later years of his life, Teilhard often spoke about the convergence of religions, but not in the sense of syncretism. In a realistic appraisal he affirmed that religious diversity is here to stay, just as racial and cultural diversity are. But our understanding and coming to terms with these differences must develop along new lines and lead to new attitudes. The idea of the convergence of religions is the opposite of an attitude that assumes that all religions are already one in their essence, that they already share the unity of a common ground that underlies all differences. Unity is not pregiven; it is not reducible to something already there. Like all living things, it has to grow and take shape over time. True convergence means the presence of an overall orientation, an axis along which certain developments of major importance occur. Like other religious thinkers, Teilhard used the image of the tree and its branches for the different religions but, unlike others, he did not interpret this image as expressing the essential sameness of all religions. For him the different branches of a tree are not all alike but differ in their form and importance. The growth of a tree advances mainly through a central stem, a trunk, but the branches have their relative points of growth too. Thus both differentiation and unity exist, and there are major lines of development.

Such terms as "the convergence of religions," "the religion of tomorrow," or "a new mysticism," found particularly in Teilhard's later writings, indicate his emphasis on the need for a reinterpretation of our traditional religious heritage. Teilhard attempted the outlines of such a reinterpretation for his own religion, Christianity, which he wanted to see extend itself to its utmost limits by surpassing itself. Looking for seeds of a religious renewal and a spirituality commensurate with the deepest aspirations of the modern world, he ultimately felt that such a renewal could not be achieved without a perspective of convergence. Speaking from a Christian point of view, Teilhard saw Christ Omega as humanity's spiritual pole and its final point of convergence. However, people from other faiths may use quite a different symbol to express both the movement and the summit of convergence. What is perhaps more important in understanding Teilhard's convergent perspective is the fact that in his numerous discussions of the human phenomenon and its future, he assigned an absolutely central place to religion. At the heart of all religions, at their focal point, lies the phenomenon of mysticism, the fountainhead of all faith and the source of all renewal.

It was such a vision of faith embracing the highest hope and the greatest love that Teilhard de Chardin wanted to communicate to his contemporaries. He wanted people to see more, for to see more means to be more, to lead a richer, more resourceful inner and outer life. In the modern situation of turmoil and crisis, he stressed the urgent need for an ever greater faith. Without it we shall not possess the necessary spiritual energy resources to build an adequate human future for all. In his inaugural address to the French branch of the World Congress of Faiths, given in 1947, he stressed the fact that the starting point for our coming together is a shared "faith in man," in the potential of human beings. This provides us with a basis, a foundation on which to build a greater unity and by which to bridge our differences. The ultimate unity found at the summit is for Teilhard the faith in God or, as others might say, faith in a transcendent Reality, and it is towards this that we have to move together.

The American theologian Robley Edward Whitson has studied the implications of contemporary cultural and religious convergence in his thought-provoking book *The Coming Convergence of World Religions*.[2] He boldly asks the question, Can any religious tradition remain separate today and survive? Apart from a few rare exceptions, we have had only a superficial and external encounter of religions so far. What will happen if dialogue-in-depth becomes more widely practiced and a more convergent perspective begins to challenge the intellectual and spiritual isolation of peoples? The religious traditions will have to continue their development together. In Whitson's words:

> They have a *further meaning together* which we had not even suspected. It is not that we will discover that all along they really were all the same. On the contrary, we must expect to find that their differences . . . are actually meaningful together, contribute to each other and constitute the new unity out of their diversity.[3]

Such a movement of convergence implies a "unitive pluralism" which creatively combines individual particularity with shared universality. In other words, beneath external differences and institutional separateness a unitary and differentiated, but not uniform, belief system can be seen to develop through the search for values we might want to share.

There is another, more compelling way of relating to each other, and that is through religious experience. On one hand, one can consider the world religions as different systems of beliefs containing widely varied forms of intellectual expression and numerous kinds of worship and ritual. On the other hand, all religions contain pointers towards the nonconceptual and nondiscursive quality of religious experience, the richness and depth of which cannot be encompassed by the limitations of language. Such experience implies a revelational character, a disclosure situation that demands the human response of faith. The quality of faith, its inner light, and its peculiar kind of certainty in the dark of life, is often linked to the sense of an Ultimate Reality, the glory of which transcends all human achievements. Yet at the same time it is experienced as a presence closer to our joys, sorrows, and sufferings than we are to ourselves. Such a vision of faith has been seen, felt, and expressed all over the globe, at all times and places, in all cultures, in all religions. It is a vision that transcends all boundaries and relates the world faiths at their center. It is a dynamic and inspiring force that can bind us together beyond all divisions. As a Hindu woman said to me once, "Ultimately, it is only faith which gives meaning to life."

The great religions are ways that have been charted for us; they remain avenues to be explored. Their teachings point to ways of life and goals of realization, but if they do not eventually lead us to such a vision of faith, their road remains incomplete, their promise unfulfilled. The difference between the external, institutional religion and the internal, essential faith element at the core can be sensed by comparing the view of a stained glass window from the outside to the view from the inside. Without entering the cathedral, one will never be able to have more than a faint perception of the great beauty, unity, and coherence that the stained glass window and its many scenes present to the insider. Extending this comparison, one may say that one can never behold the vision of faith from the externals of religion. The view from inside the cathedral, the synagogue, the mosque, the temple, the vihara, and gurdwara is always quite unlike that which one gets by merely contemplating the external building.

We have explored certain aspects of convergence and said that unity can be found through the shared experience of faith. William Johnston writes in his study *The Inner Eye of Love*, which deals with convergent aspects of Christianity and Buddhism:

> We constantly hear talk about the crisis of faith in the modern world. But . . . our crisis is not one of faith but of belief. What is called into question today is the cultural superstructure with its myriad of beliefs. But there is plenty of evidence to support the view that the inner light of faith is as strong as ever in the modern world . . . while the great religions differ in their beliefs, their members can be deeply united in faith.[4]

One might say that, in a way, we have to go beyond belief to the center of religion, to faith.

### 3. What Can World Faiths Contribute to the Convergence of Humankind?

I would like to argue that the contribution of the world faiths is essential; in fact, it seems indispensable if humankind ever wants to achieve greater unity and integration. Without a vision of faith we shall never overcome our competitive greed; we shall never find true peace, and we will never experience the all-transforming powers of love. For it is love alone, freely offered and generously given, which forges the strongest bonds. I would like to emphasize the dynamic and active quality of love. We hear so much about the need to be loved for a child to grow, a person to mature, a marriage to work, and for people to get along together. But it is even more important to stress the need to teach and learn to practice love, to love in the active rather than the passive mode.

To learn to love means to overcome the limitations of one's own self-centeredness by being centered on others. This is the most essential and dynamic element which the world faiths can contribute to the making of human beings and the creation of a juster world. All religions call for a change of heart and preach the need for a profound transformation of self. Some express this passively as self-surrender or negation of self; others put it actively as sacrificial love or submission to the will of God. In whatever mode expressed, it indicates the possibility of a deep change in the human personality and presents a challenging summons to a richer and more authentic way of life. One can speak of an essential characteristic of spiritual life, as Gaston Berger has done, and see it "as a force, a march, a movement towards being, towards light, towards salvation. It is only interesting to get to know the details of the itineraries, of the customs, of the ceremonies, if one has first conceived a longing for the great adventure."[5]

The search for a great adventure haunts many of our contemporaries, but it can take strange and perverse forms, sometimes leading not to greater, but to lesser, being. The two most significant aspects of contemporary civilization may be characterized as follows: There is on the one hand the emergence of a new world culture which overcomes traditional differences and transcends the separateness of East and West. This new culture has global dimensions, and all cultural and religious traditions are contributing towards its growth. On the other hand, there also exists quite a new emphasis on the place of inwardness in human life. A new sense of adventure is growing, concerned with exploring the different layers of consciousness and piercing through to undreamed of levels of depth, of interiority. Both these movements are worldwide, and are slowly permeating all levels of society.

The development of religion and society are always closely interrelated. Today, with a growing awareness of the existence of a global society, we need not only world citizens, but also "world believers" who are deeply rooted in their own religious heritage without being closed to that of others. This means that one can relate to one's own tradition in a self-critical manner, while being aware of and open to the faith of others, widening out to a vision of universality. This creative tension between the particular and universal was perhaps best expressed by Gandhi when he said that he wanted the windows of his house to be wide open to the winds from all corners of the earth without him being swept off his feet.

Many questions relating to the external conduct of life have found hitherto unknown solutions in modern society. However, questions of choice and meaning, of decisive priorities and values, are pressing in on us with an increasing urgency. In the past, the pursuit of religious questions, of reflections about God, the human being and the world, the nature of their relationship, as well as the question of the meaning and quality of human life, were restricted to a small number of people belonging to a social and intellectual, a monastic and mystic elite. Mass religiosity through the ages has always been of quite a different character than the religion of the official religious leaders, the religious virtuosi, the saints, the seers, the mystics. However, with the growth of a more egalitarian, participatory society, the spread of education, and especially the increasing availability of greater leisure to all, more people have access to more differentiated modes of life and thought. If they so wish, people can choose possibilities for self-development, self-fulfillment, and self-transcendence in quite a new manner. Religious experience has, so to speak, become democratized; it has become a new live option because it is open to more people in modern society, and it has become itself more open, more universal. In this sense the vision of oneness seen by the mystics and saints of all religions, the message of a universal brotherhood and sisterhood of humankind, can also become more fully embodied in society and assume a greater social reality than in previous periods of history.

It is against this background of a profound social change that one must see the contribution of the world faiths in a new light. We require a dynamic, an essentially modern approach to religion, with a primary concern for the present, the here and now. Concrete solutions to our current problems can hardly be expected to exist in the past. What is needed most of all is a truly creative exercise of the religious imagination in our approach to humanity's religious heritage. But we need more than a new interpretation of the multiplicity of the living religions.

We need a new religious breakthrough in our understanding of faith as a core element of being human, and in our practice of spiritualilty in a situation of cultural convergence and greater social interaction. Many religious thinkers have stressed and are stressing this need for a new kind of spirituality. Berdyayev wrote about it in the thirties, as did Teilhard de Chardin, but Radhakrishnan, Aurobindo, and Iqbal, to mention only a few who are considered to be "modernizers" within their own religious tradition, have also emphasized the need for a contemporary spirituality.

Not all past religious beliefs and practices are of equal importance for the development of an adequate contemporary spirituality, and this is true in all religious traditions. We have to explore the meaning of religion and spirituality in an encounter situation and ask, What is real in religion? What is the heart of religion? What is its center? Religions in East and West have traditionally given different answers to this, and one can legitimately speak about a plurality of centers. Yet there must also be a search for a higher center wherein we can relate to each other beyond the diversity of our standpoints. If we can find such a center of religion, this may help us to find the center of ourselves.

There is much talk of centering, of the need for an inner ecology, the restoration of inwardness as well as the expansion of consciousness. This is partly a reaction against society at large, which is mainly concerned with impersonal processes such as politics, economy, industry, education, health, and development. It is often felt that only a radical reorientation in our focus of attention from the impersonal to the person, to human beings and their growth, will bring about a better society. In the religious sphere there is a parallel situation in that one can observe an important shift away from religious institutions to the personal and experiential element in religion. The important and decisive role of mysticism for the future of religion seems to be undeniable. But this mysticism must not be understood as merely an inwardness sought and found apart from the world, an emotional escape route towards inner peace and solace. On the contrary, it is a mysticism which feeds back into social action.

The future of religion lies in the interdependent development of inner awareness with outer activity, in the simultaneous growth of both the personal and social sphere. Their transformation can only occur together, and it is in this sense that some writers speak of a "mysticism of action" or a "mysticism of shared endeavor." A faith which is alive will grow and expand; its vision will have room for others and their point of view. Understood in this sense, religion can foster the process of individuation and achieve growth and integration for the individual, but it can also help towards better social integration. Traditional spirituality has arrived at an important crossroads where either a new religious vision will emerge, or religions will stagnate and finally die out. This is bound to happen if we cannot separate the ossified from the living tradition.

The encounter of religions in the modern world has come about through the situation of cultural convergence. One hears much talk about interreligious dialogue, even trialogue, and multilogue, which implies the speech of many voices. Some of them, alas, sound more cacophonous than harmonious. But there is certainly a more open climate of thought, a greater willingness to listen to and learn from each other, a growing openness to faiths other than one's own, which represents a new threshold in interreligious relations.

We are in the fortunate position of living in a multi-cultural, multi-ethnic, and multi-religious society. One need not travel far today to encounter world faiths in all their diversity. Some are still too frightened of this new situation and consider other ways of life and thinking as a threat to their own. I see the diversity of faiths as an enriching experience, accompanied by creative tension in that it questions our easily assumed identities and our false securities. This is a new stage of the religious quest which asks for a positive response. From diverse origins we are beginning to move towards a unitive center of convergence. This movement has been best characterized by R.E. Whitson when he writes:

> Each of the world religions is unique and universal: unique in that the core of each is a distinct central experience . . . not to be found

elsewhere, and universal in that this core experience is of supreme significance for all men. It is the ability of a tradition of religious experience to speak to other men that calls us to recognize it as a world religion... There is no way to argue through to an understanding of the impact of convergence. It must be felt. If it is, then this experience will lead us to the realistic understanding of convergence... To be willing to experience demands much of us, especially as this unfolding experience is new. We fear the insecurity implicit in a new experience and this betrays our innermost temptation to infidelity: we want the experience of the sacred to make us feel secure—we do not want the consciousness that the mighty acts of God must be our acts, our creativity, our responsibility.[6]

To achieve convergence, we have to meet each other, we have to talk to each other. But this is not enough if we do not learn to accept and ultimately to love each other. Dialogue-in-depth implies an existential commitment and participation which transforms the partners involved. The most important elements and the most precious heritage of the living religions will have to be related and assessed in terms of each other. Thus we can foresee a new convergent development whereby the world faiths relate meaningfully to each other and discover new dimensions and riches together.

Many religious traditions use the image of different paths leading to the same summit. It symbolically expresses the diversity of man's religious quest as well as the unity of its goal. The summit presents a challenge, and it implies a choice. We can reach a unity of convergence if we keep the vision of the summit as a goal before our eyes.

# 8

## Teilhard's Association with the World Congress of Faiths, 1947-1950

Today there is a greater awareness of the need for interreligious encounter and dialogue than ever before. Many individuals and organizations are exploring insights of faiths other than their own and are seeking to promote understanding between different religions. This was not always so and even a few decades ago the climate of encounter was far less open than at present. One organization which pioneered interreligious dialogue and has been active in it for over fifty years is the World Congress of Faiths (WCF).

It is not generally known that Teilhard de Chardin, after his return from China in May 1946, was associated with the activities of the French branch of the World Congress of Faiths, for which he wrote several talks and lectures. The World Congress of Faiths was founded in England in 1936 at the initiative of Sir Francis Younghusband and is still active in promoting interreligious encounter and dialogue today. From the beginning, certain Frenchmen, particularly the well-known scholar of Islamic studies, Louis Massignon, and the orientalist, Jacques Bacot, showed great interest in this interreligious movement, which aims "to break down the barrier of exclusivism and to build bridges between faiths."[1] After three congresses had taken place in London (1936), Oxford (1937), and Cambridge (1938), the French organized the next congress as a joint meeting in Paris (the Sorbonne, July 5-10, 1939). However, because of the outbreak of World War II soon afterwards, no further activity occurred, and the official founding of a French branch did not take place until 1947.

The French called their branch *Le Congrès Universel des Croyants* and renamed it later simply *Union des Croyants.* Its founding members were all actively engaged in the study of the history of religions, or of Eastern religions and art. They were René Grousset, then director of the oriental museum in Paris, the *Musée Cernuschi*; Louis Massignon; Paul Masson-Oursel; H.C. Puech; and Georges Salles. The president was the orientalist Jacques Bacot [2] and the general secretaries were Madame Béatrice d'Hauteville and Madame Solange Lemaître. [3] It was probably through meeting the latter that Teilhard first learned about the plan for founding a French branch of the World Congress of Faiths. The Council members of the French branch included, among others, an Iranian Sufi, a Confucian, the Hindu Swami Siddheswarananda from the Ramakrishna Mission, and the French philosophers, Etienne Gilson, Gabriel Marcel, and Edouard Le Roy, with whom Teilhard had been closely associated between 1921 and 1930. [4]

Teilhard's biographer, Claude Cuénot, briefly mentions that the World Congress of Faiths became a useful field of activities for Teilhard during his stay in Paris, 1946-1951, but he goes on to say that "although he could not actively and officially co-operate, he was anxious to encourage the movement for unity." [5] Judging from different accounts, Teilhard seems to have been quite an active member, although it is not easy to determine his exact relationship to the Congress as the French branch did not have membership contributions at the time. Jacques Bacot speaks of Teilhard as a "guest and adviser who contributed all his ardour" [6] to the work of the association, and one of the general secretaries confirmed that Teilhard was present at many committee meetings. [7]

It seems certain that Teilhard had many discussions with different members of the French branch of the World Congress of Faiths. Particularly the friendship with René Grousset and

Madame Lemaître provided him with a welcome opportunity to clarify and express more succinctly some of his ideas on the phenomenon of religion. Moreover, their meetings may have made him realize some of his own shortcomings, particularly regarding his understanding of Eastern religions. It is here that the exchange with René Grousset proved to be especially important, for Grousset's writings led Teilhard to a closer study of comparative mysticism. Teilhard worked at the library of the Musée Guimet during this time and, in 1948, he also attended the Orientalists' Congress.[8] Cuénot believes that "talking with Grousset helped Teilhard to see more clearly the implications of the religious currents he had become familiar with in the East."[9] The outcome of these clarifications was Teilhard's essay "The Spiritual Contribution of the Far East," written in February 1947. It reflects a greater awareness of and openness to the Eastern religious traditions than some of Teilhard's earlier writings. However, this essay was not written for the World Congress of Faiths, and, therefore, does not directly enter into the present discussion.[10]

Between 1947 and 1950, Teilhard wrote five direct contributions for the French branch of the World Congress of Faiths and took part in a discussion which is available in cyclostyled form. Four of these contributions are now published in Teilhard's collected works. But as they are not always listed as talks to the World Congress of Faiths, I shall first list all contributions in chronological order and then analyze their content, which suggests that Teilhard's activities for the World Congress of Faiths, and the whole Parisian milieu in which he was working then, led him to certain reflections on the phenomenon of religion which helped him to articulate earlier intuitions more clearly.

The following list of Teilhard's contributions to the World Congress of Faiths indicates first the date and title of each essay in French, together with the number of the volume in the *Collected Works* [Editions du Seuil] in which it can be found, followed by the published English translation, where available.[11]

1. March 8, 1947 – *"La foi en l'homme,"* Vol. V, pp. 235-43.
    English translation: "Faith in Man," in *The Future of Man,*

Collins, 1965, pp. 185-192.

2. July 2-4, 1948 — Paris meeting of the World Congress of Faiths, with the participation of English and Dutch delegates. Three papers were given by Eric Palmstierna, Louis Massignon, and René Grousset. Teilhard participated in the discussion on July 3, 1948; the other participants were Lady Ravensdale, Aldous Huxley, Paul Masson-Oursel, H. Ch. Puech, and Gabriel Marcel. The discussion is only available in cyclostyled form.

3. January 29, 1949 — *"La Peur Existentielle,"* published under the title *"Un phénomène de contre-évolution en biologie humaine ou la peur de l'existence,"* Vol. VII, pp. 187-202. English translation: "A Phenomenon of Counter-Evolution in Human Biology," in *Activation of Energy*, Collins, 1970, pp. 181-195.

4. January 21, 1950 — *"Comment concevoir et espérer que se réalise sur terre une unanimité humaine?"*, Vol. V, pp. 367-374. English translation: "How May We Conceive and Hope that Human Unanimisation Will Be Realised on Earth?", in *The Future of Man*, 1965, pp. 281-88.

5. September, 1950 — *"Le Congrès Universel des Croyants,"*, two pages describing the aims of the World Congress of Faiths. Unpublished.

6. December 9, 1950 — *"Le goût de vivre,"* Vol. VII, pp. 237-51. English translation: "The Zest for Living," in *Activation of Energy*, Collins, 1970, pp. 229-43.

I shall now look at each of these contributions in turn.

*1.* The inaugural session of the French branch of the World Congress of Faiths took place on March 8, 1947. Teilhard was not personally present, but at the request of the Congress, he wrote an inaugural address which was read by René Grousset. It revolves around the theme that people of different backgrounds and convictions can come together and cooperate through their common "faith in man." This faith is defined as "the more or less active and fervent conviction that Mankind as an organic and organised whole possesses a future," a future which, beyond mere survival, means some form of higher life.[12] The essentially modern concepts of collectivity and of an organic future have led to an awakening and transformation of human consciousness which has also brought with it a spiritual crisis on an unprecedented scale. After discussing the ambiguity of this situation, Teilhard outlines some of the forces that may unite humankind:

A tendency towards unification is everywhere manifest, and especially in the different branches of religion. We are looking for something that will draw us together, below or above the level of that which divides... Not through external pressure but only from an inward impulse can the unity of Mankind endure and grow. And this, it seems, is where the major, "providential" role reserved by the future for what we have called "faith in Man" displays itself. A profound common aspiration arising out of the very shape of the modern world...

Later he says:

In short, we may say that faith in Man... shows itself upon examination to be the general atmosphere in which the higher, more elaborated forms of faith which we all hold in one way or another may best (indeed can only) grow and come together...

No one doubts that we are all more or less affected by this elementary, primordial faith. Should we otherwise truly belong to our time? ...I have said that the spirit has only one summit. But it has also only one basis. Let us look well and we shall find that our Faith in God, detached as it may be, sublimates in us a rising tide of human aspirations. It is to this original sap that we must return if we wish to communicate with the brothers with whom we seek to be united.[13]

With these words the inaugural address concludes. Fifteen years later, looking back at the development of the French branch of the World Congress of Faiths, Louis Massignon called this address "an outstanding text" which from the start provided a direction for the work of the World Congress of Faiths.[14]

Thematically, the text is closely linked to the short paper "Ecumenism"[15], which Teilhard had written three months before, on December 15, 1946. There he had clearly distinguished between two kinds of ecumenism: the ultimate one at the summit which, however, cannot be reached without a previous ecumenism at the base. The latter tries to develop the foundation of a common human faith in the future of humanity.

Earlier still, in March 1941, in remarks to a Congress in Science and Religion, Teilhard had attempted to outline the "possible bases of a universal human creed" which he presented as the personal testimony "of thirty years spent in close and sincere contact with scientific and religious circles in Europe, America, and the Far East."[16] Though less clearly stated, we find the same ideas expressed: a rightly understood faith in the future, and the idea of a possible awakening of a higher state of consciousness are both seen as necessary for preserving in human beings the taste for action. What is more, they alone are capable of bringing about that necessary synthesis of adoration wherein people can combine "both a passionate desire to conquer the World and a passionate longing to be united with God."[17]

Thus we have a theme here which forms an integral and essential part of Teilhard's view of the world and his understanding of religion. Earlier this theme was expressed as the necessary integration of two kinds of faith, the faith in God ahead and the faith in God above, the immanent God of evolution and the transcendent God. Now the theme has, so to speak, left the theological circle and become universalized. Speaking to people of different religious traditions and no tradition at all, Teilhard emphasizes faith in man, the world, the future, as a common bond. Faith in the human being is the uniting basis for a humanity seeking the spirit at its summit. The conclusion of 1947 still echoes the motto of the very first lines Teilhard ever wrote: "There is a communion with God, and a communion with earth, and a communion with God through earth" (1916).[18] The continuity and persistence of this insight, which endured for some thirty years, is truly remarkable.

*2.* There is evidence that Teilhard took an active part in the various activities of the French branch of the World Congress of Faiths during the year 1948. He sometimes edited papers presented by foreigners unskilled in French and participated in discussions with various members of the World Congress of Faiths.[19] The only record of one such discussion is the cyclostyled text of a meeting on July 3, 1948. During exchanges with Louis Massignon and Gabriel Marcel, Teilhard stressed on one hand the importance of a faith and the necessity to recognize the right to a faith in others, and on the other hand, the need for cooperation with all those who do not adhere to any particular faith at all. He recognized the possibililty of a coming together, a development of convergent lines, with contributions from all sides. Similarly, he stressed his quite different understanding of mysticism and the need to renew the mysticism of the West. In his view, the West "has not yet found its formula of faith" which answers the need of the present. Within humankind a faith and mysticism may develop which presently do not yet exist.[20]

*3.* The next contribution was a talk about "existential fear," which he gave to a group of members of the World Congress of Faiths. This talk is not concerned with religion as such; rather, it analyzes the general human predicament and also a particular historical situation. Given in postwar Paris in 1949, it indirectly counterbalances the nihilistic tendencies of some of the French existentialist philosophers. Teilhard vividly described his contemporaries' existential anguish and analyzed the historical, psychological, and social reasons to which it is due. There is, however, a message of hope: there can be a reversal of this existential fear if human beings can develop trust, peace, and love, if they can see the world is converging.

I quote from his talk:

> The universe . . . crushes us in the first place . . . by the impact of its blind immensity; this is because, as in a forest or in a big city, we feel that we count for nothing in it; we can only trail along like lost souls. On the other hand, however, the forest and the big city—and nature herself—lose their horror and arouse love the

moment we recognize around us a *radiating* system of paths, or roads, or lines of evolution, and so feel certain that, however thick the undergrowth may be, however inhospitable the district, however dark the life we are passing through, warmth and friendship and shelter are waiting for us at the centre of the star—and that we can no longer lose our way to them . . .

Thus the experience is completley changed from one of anxiety into one of reassurance:

The universe was dark, icy and blind; now it lights up, becomes warm, and is animated. As though by magic, our terror of matter and man is transformed, is reversed, into *peace and assurance* – and even . . . *into existential love.* At last we have emerged from the labyrinth. We have escaped from our agony. We are made free. *And all this because the world has a heart.*[21]

*4.* The fourth contribution centers around the question of how a greater human unity or a unification of humankind may be achieved. There are many external forces at work to bring people closer together, but this is not enough. Only a free unification based on mutual attraction and love can lead to the true union of human beings; for this some form of affective energy is needed. Beyond the "push" of external forces, a "pull" towards "something" is needed and Teilhard sees this pull as coming from a point of universal convergence in the future. After the emergence of life, and then the growth of critical reflection, a third important threshold is now in view, the building-up of one human community. The Marxist view sees the human collectivity in terms of a merely human future; the Christian view sees the center of universal convergence as both ultrahuman and transcendent. It has the warmth of attraction of personal love as its summit: ". . . it seems that Man's urge towards *Some Thing* ahead of him cannot achieve its full fruition except by combining with another and still more fundamental aspiration—one from above, urging him towards *Some One.*"[22]

*5.* The search for *Some Thing* (or *Some One*) ahead is expressed again in the brief unpublished description of the aims of the

World Congress of Faiths, given in two pages dated September 1950. Here again the need for some principle of unification is stated, such as the birth of some common spirit, the awakening of faith in life, for without it the forces of collectivity will break and harden people. Teilhard sees it as one of the aims of the World Congress of Faiths to help work out such a faith which allows people to become one with others.

There is no question of the World Congress of Faiths proclaiming the essential sameness of all religions, nor does it wish to reject any purely human creed. Rather, the World Congress of Faiths movement represents an effort to bring together in some way all those who believe:

a. that there is a future and a way out for the world ahead of us;

b. that this very future and way out depend in fact on the union of all individuals, races, and nations of the world, which, one day, will have to come about on our planet;

c. that this union, however much conditioned by technical and social progress, can only be accomplished through the vision and influence of a supreme center of attraction and personalization.

The work is based on two fundamental convictions. Everything that rises beyond itself through the love of something greater will, in fact, converge towards a summit. At present, an immense number of isolated elements in the human community already seek to rise and come together, but Teilhard envisages the growth of sympathy and attraction on a scale unknown in the past that will bring people much closer together.

It is important for people to meet and to get to know each other to bring about such a rapprochement. The different types of scientific thought and religious faith found in the world today have to come into contact with each other and further develop in reaction to each other. Only then may human beings finally discover *Some Thing* (or *Some One*) ahead.

Here again Teilhard speaks in general terms, without any specific reference to particular religions. In fact, the term *religion* or *religious faith* is very little used. There are other forces at work which can bring people initially together; it is the "ecumenism at the base," as he calls it elsewhere, which needs to be pursued first in order to bring about understanding and unification. Religions cannot achieve this human unity on their own, but they must contribute towards it and, what is more, without the deepest intuitions of the great religious traditions, human efforts of sympathy and union cannot find their true center. This is very clearly and specifically stated in the last contribution to the work of the World Congress of Faiths, the essay "The Zest for Living," written on December 9, 1950, three months after the brief statement on the aims of the movement.

6. In the first two parts of this essay Teilhard describes in a general way the character and importance of this *goût de vivre*—the will to live and love life, a dynamic, constructive, and adventurous quality, indispensable for the continuity of life and the development of a higher life. This relates to Teilhard's frequently repeated warning that the enemy number one today is indifference and boredom—a certain *taedium vitae* reflecting the loss of just such a taste for life and the absence of inner resources. At the deepest level, the zest for life is thus linked to an act of faith:

> . . . what is most vitally necessary to the thinking earth is a faith — and a great faith — and ever more faith.
>
> To know that we are not prisoners.
>
> To know that there is a way out, that there is air, and light and love, somewhere, beyond the reach of all death.
>
> To know this, to know that it is neither an illusion nor a fairy tale. — That, if we are not to perish smothered in the very stuff of our being, is what we must at all costs secure. And it is there that we find what I may well be so bold as to call the *evolutionary role* of religions.[23]

This notion of the evolutionary role of religions is an important one: religions have a contribution to make to the further development of the human community. The third part of the essay discusses, therefore, what we may expect from the combined effort of religions. The nineteenth century may have been misled into believing that the age of religions had passed. It is certain that the profound influence of science is refashioning creeds and beliefs but without being exclusively destructive: "The forces of religion are emerging from the ordeal they have just gone through" and are more important than ever before for the supply of human mental and spiritual energy. The "reserves of faith" so necessary for the construction of the future must continually increase. However, it is important to realize that contemporary religious needs are not the same as in the past. A historically new situation has created a new awareness which asks for a new spirituality and a new image of God.[24]

A spirituality for the individual alone is no longer enough. Teilhard speaks of "a religion of mankind and the earth." Contemporary religious needs can only be answered by those mystical currents which are able to combine the traditional faith in the above (that is, flight from the world, from the bonds of time, to union with some Absolute) with the newborn faith in some issue ahead (that is, integration into a human community and union with others, and the unity found together in a higher center).

Why, then, not have a completely new faith based on some "evolutionary sense" or "sense of man"? Teilhard lists two reasons that this would not be a satisfactory solution:

> First of all, there can be no doubt that in each of the great religious branches that cover the world at this moment, a certain spiritual attitude and vision which have been produced by centuries of experience are preserved and continued; these are as indispensable and irreplaceable for the integrity of a total terrestrial religious consciousness as the various "racial" components . . .
>
> This, however, is not all. What is carried along by the various currents of faith that are still active on the earth, working in their incommunicable core, is no longer only the irreplaceable elements of a certain complete image of the universe. Very much more even than *fragments of vision*, it is *experiences of contact* with a supreme Ineffable which they preserve and pass on.[25]

The most important idea contained in these paragraphs is Teilhard's recognition of the diversity and complementarity of the "active currents of faiths," what we today would call the "living religious traditions." Each of them contains fragments of vision and experiences of contact with a supreme Ineffable. It is only the sum total of these visions and experiences which represents the full religious heritage of humankind, and this heritage is most precious for the development of a "total terrestrial religious consciousness," necessary for a humanity that wants to be one. It is at this source that the deepest springs of human energy dwell and therefore these active currents of faiths are of prime importance in maintaining the zest for living: ". . . sustained and guided by the tradition of the great human mysticisms, we succeed, through contemplation and prayer, in entering directly into receptive communication with the very source of all inner drive (élan)."[26]

Of all the contributions written for the World Congress of Faiths, this one deals most explicitly with the understanding of the role of religions in the contemporary world. It also implies the need for a closer contact and dialogue between the different religious traditions and thus it well befits the aims for which a movement such as the World Congress of Faiths is working.

Further indirect influences of Teilhard's association with the French branch of the World Congress of Faiths may be discerned here and there in essays of this period, in some of the correspondence, especially in the important exchanges with Madame Solange Lemaître, and in his diary entries of 1947-51. I have undertaken a fuller analysis of this partly unpublished material elsewhere.[27] This chapter merely wishes to document Teilhard's close link with certain members and activities of the French branch of the World Congress of Faiths after his return from China in order to provide an accurate historical record which gives clear evidence of his early support for the encounter and dialogue between people of different faiths.

# Teilhard's Comparison of Western and Eastern Mysticism

Teilhard de Chardin lived for many years in the East. As a young man he spent three years teaching in Egypt (1905-1908) and later he worked for over twenty years in China (1923-1946) where he traveled widely. He also spent several months in Burma and India and made brief visits to Java and Japan. During his extensive travels he certainly came into contact with adherents of Buddhism, Hinduism, Islam, and Chinese religions. On first inspection, however, his writings on religion and mysticism appear to make little direct reference to Eastern religions, and what reference there is would seem to show a certain lack of empathy and an unjustifiable underrating of Eastern traditions in comparison with his own Western religious experience.

Can this initial impression be shown to be correct when one scrutinizes his writings more closely? More than one passage can be cited demonstrating Teilhard's attraction to Eastern thought. For example:

. . . my own individual faith was inevitably peculiarly sensitive to Eastern influences; and I am perfectly conscious of having felt their attraction. . . Thus the East fascinates me by its faith in the ultimate unity of the universe; but the fact remains that the two of us, the

> East and I, have two diametrically opposed conceptions of the relationship by which there is commmunication between the totality and its elements. For the East, the One is seen as a suppression of the multiple; for me, the One is born from the concentration of the multiple. Thus, under the same monist appearances, there are two moral systems, two metaphysics and two mysticisms.[1]

This passage stresses the importance of a faith in ultimate unity, but it also highlights the principle of difference which Teilhard sees as decisive between Eastern spirituality and his own. Two of his essays that deal explicitly with a comparison between Western and Eastern mysticism are found in his book *Toward the Future*[2] and are entitled "The Road of the West: To a New Mysticism" (1932)[3] and "The Spiritual Contribution of the Far East: Some Personal Reflections" (1947).[4] They contain perhaps little that is intrinsically new for someone familiar with Teilhard's views on the comparison between East and West; yet they have the advantage of presenting this comparison in a systematic form and in adducing certain modifications in what many an interpreter has thought to be too harsh a judgment on Eastern religions.

For a complete analysis of Teilhard's attitudes to Eastern religions and to mysticism in general, it is necessary to trace his direct experience of the East and its different religions, and to uncover, as far as possible, earlier indirect contacts with the East that may have contributed to the formation of these attitudes. Thus there is the *historical-factual problem* of finding out about Teilhard's knowledge and experience of Eastern religions. Then there is the *genetic problem* of how his ideas about Eastern religions were formed and evolved through meeting adherents of particular religions or through further reading and reflection. Were Teilhard's own religious and mystic experiences merely expressed in traditional Christian modes of thought, or did he, after passing through sucessive and tentative formulations, eventually go beyond his own religious tradition and transcend it in some way? If so, what contribution may the experience of Eastern religions and the resulting reflection on this experience have made to this synthesizing process?

This is not the place to pursue these questions as I have

undertaken a wider study of these questions elsewhere.[5] Here I shall confine myself to a presentation and critical discussion of the ideas contained in the two comparative essays mentioned above. They deserve a detailed investigation on their own, and we shall look at each of them in turn, showing which experiences, encounters, and exchanges of ideas caused Teilhard to arrive at the views expressed in these essays. We also have to consider how best to understand these views from our contemporary experience of greater global convergence between East and West.

## "THE ROAD OF THE WEST – TO A NEW MYSTICISM" (1932)

The essay begins with the contention that there is no religion without mysticism, and there is no mysticism without faith in unity. Teilhard wants to show how humankind today, under new conditions and especially under the influence of modern science, is trying to find a new spirituality which leads to a higher and fuller unity. This spirituality develops in continuity with, but also in opposition to, the ancient mysticisms, especially the oriental ones.

The discussion then proceeds in three stages. First the "Oriental Path" is briefly treated. After a short reference to the earlier ethnological controversies about the origin of religion, Teilhard says that the true beginnings of mysticism cannot be found with primitive man: "Pre-logic . . . knows only a pre-religion and a pre-mysticism."[6] True mysticism was first born in India five or ten centuries before the Christian era. Teilhard speaks of a mystic "cyclone" in the plains of the Ganges which made India for a long time the religious pole of the earth. Without going into the historical details regarding the divergent views of particular Indian schools or teachers, Teilhard sees as the major characteristic of the oriental way, or the "road of the East," as he calls it elsewhere, that unity is achieved through release or return, through identification with an underlying ground and not through union with a higher center. Unity is reached by withdrawing from, negating, and ultimately destroying the multiple. This attitude denies any *real* value to this world and is "the complete death of constructive activity: the radical emptiness of the experimental universe."[7] Other texts emphasize that constructive activity and effort are needed for the further evolution of the human being and the world which the study of the course of past evolutionary history posits as likely. The stage of possible further self-evolution which we have reached now cannot be based on values of denial and withdrawal.

Even when speaking in 1932 about Western interest in Neo-Buddhism and oriental religions, Teilhard thought he could sometimes detect, among other more positive signs, a certain disdain for the world and its real values. The confusing state of multiplicity is fled, and unity is found through the suppression of the multiple itself. But Teilhard could also perceive the outlines of an occidental neo-mysticism pointing towards another direction. This "Occidental Path" is discussed in the second part of the essay. Here the solution to the problem of unity is seen as diametrically opposed to the monist solution. The experimental universe is considered as a whole formed out of interlinked elements which can be brought more closely together through an internal gathering up. Unity is created through the union of all the elements which is effected over time. Here the multiple is no longer reduced to an underlying common ground, but a new unity is brought about through the gradual transformation and convergence of multiple elements. This process cannot be understood as cyclic or linear; its most adequate image is the slowly mounting spiral which Teilhard uses elsewhere to express the dynamism and direction of this convergence. "Heaven is not opposed to the earth but it is born from the conquest and transformation of the earth. God is not reached through extenuation but through sublimation."[8] It is this effort to reach *beyond* and not below consciousness, to realize a higher personalization and not to dissolve personality in general cosmic consciousness, which the author sees as the most distinguishing feature of the "road of the West."

Teilhard's own "passion for the Absolute" (as he describes it so aptly in his autobiographical essay "The Heart of the Matter"), his unceasing quest for the One, culminated in the search for God in and through all the elements of the universe which he experienced as a "communion with God through the earth." Two traditionally exclusive attitudes are combined into one new synthesis which he judges to be the great religious discovery of modern times. This new orientation will transform traditional Christianity as much as Islam or Buddhism. A closer coming together of the different religions may be possible through the adoption of this converging view by all living religious traditons. "There can no longer be any question . . . of setting up a simple opposition between one and multiple, between spirit and matter. Each must be sought out and worshipped through the other . . . The unity of the world is based on construction and effort—it tends towards concentration and not release."[9]

Spirituality is in an entirely *new* way closely related to the development of the tangible world itself. In the past, religions were primarily linked to individual needs and hopes, or to national and racial movements. Today humankind is experiencing itself as one in a sense unknown before. The need for world unity and the necessary action to bring it about can ultimately only be inspired by a single soul. Thus the new mysticism is no longer related only to the spiritual development of the individual, but to that of the entire world as well. Despite his frequent and sometimes sharp criticism of contemporary Christianity, Teilhard sees this new mysticism as growing out of the central stem of Christianity.

This theme is especially discussed in the third part of the essay entitled "Occidental Mysticism and Christianity." The occidental way or new mysticism appears as a prolongation of the Christian tradition. But originally Christianity was also influenced by Eastern mysticism as can be seen, for example, in the theme of renunciation or the ideal of perfection that inspired the desert fathers. Teilhard sees the entire history of Western mysticism as a long, drawn-out effort to separate these two spiritualities: the oriental way, which suppresses matter, and the occidental way, which sublimates it. The difference is very marked—these are not two components which can be harmonized into one spirituality as is sometimes thought, but they are basically two *irreconcilable attitudes*. The road of the West, as that of the East, leads through asceticism to ecstasy, but a different spirit can be perceived behind the respective ascetic attitudes: there the total escape from matter, here its transformation, while, at the same time, the primacy of the spiritual over matter, and the primacy of the personal within the spiritual, are maintained. "The Hindu saint recollects and extenuates himself in order to shake matter off his garment: the Christian saint in order to transfigure and penetrate it."[10] These two attitudes are to some extent still intermingled in Christian spirituality, but we have now arrived at an important bifurcation: the path is divided between the old track of the East, where unity is found through the negation of the multiple, and the new road of the West, where, taking all earthly values into account, unity is found through the unification of the multiple rather than its abandonment. Historically and experimentally, life seems to advance on this road of the West.

At first, Teilhard's essay "The Road of the West" can hurt in its negativity towards the "road of the East," if one understands both terms too literally. But one must not overlook that the author himself points out that his presentation of the "oriental solution" to the philosophical and ultimately mystical problem of the One and the Many is "over-simplified."[11] He is not looking for historical particulars but tries to uncover general structures in the mysticisms of the past. He also asks the highly relevant question of how far these structures are still adequate for a contemporary spirituality, whether in the East or the West.

Although Teilhard had not yet been to India when he wrote "The Road of the West" in 1932,[12] he had spent considerable time in the Far East since 1923 and had met several orientalists and specialists in Eastern religions. The reason for his being in the East was first and foremost scientific research concerned with fieldwork in paleontology and geology. However, his interest during his numerous expeditions always surpassed the mere curiosity of a superficial culture-contact with the populations he encountered. He was not only a scientist, but a profound religious thinker too who, just because of his religious ideas, had been sent into an Eastern exile by his order. Teilhard reflected on the phenomenon of religion wherever he encountered it, for it is central to his understanding of the "phenomenon of man" or the "human phenomenon," as a more accurate translation of the French *phénomène humain* should read.

Between writing "The Road of the West" and the later essay "The Spiritual Contribution of the Far East," Teilhard read the two-volume study by P. Johanns, *Vers le Christ par le Vedanta.*[13] He kept extensive notes about his reading in his *Carnet de Lecture I.* The size of a school exercise book, this *carnet* has ten pages of extracts and comments on the views of Shankara, Ramanuja, and Vallabha regarding their teachings on God and the world. It also contains notes on the role of Krishna and bhakti in Hinduism. Although these notes cannot be discussed here, they are mentioned as evidence to show that although he was not a specialist in the comparative study of religion, this area was not entirely unfamiliar to him.[14]

We know for certain that "The Road of the West" was criticized soon after its completion on September 8, 1932. Teilhard must have sent a copy of the manuscript to his friend Henri de Lubac at Lyon, whom he had known since 1922 and with whom he had been in correspondence since 1930. De Lubac had been lecturing in the history of religions at the faculty of theology in Lyon since 1931, and this teaching commitment had brought him into contact with the priest Jules Monchanin. The latter was considered an authority on Eastern religions who was so deeply attracted to Indian spirituality that he eventually founded a Christian ashram in South India. This radiated a wide influence on a number of priests and lay people interested in the encounter of Christianity and Hinduism. Abbé Monchanin met Teilhard several times in France from 1925 onwards and admired his privately circulated writings, particularly his essay "The Spirit of the Earth" (1931). De Lubac must have discussed "The Road of the West" ("*La Route de l'Ouest*") with Monchanin, and reports that the latter found this essay more questionable than Teilhard's earlier works.[15] De Lubac transmitted these criticisms to Teilhard, to which he replied on October 8, 1933, saying:

> I was most interested in your friendly criticisms of "*La Route de l'Ouest*". But, if I am not mistaken, they prove precisely the

importance of what I tried to show . . . I fully allow the alternation of detachment and attachment (cf. *Le milieu divin.*) But I believe that it is in the particular, *specific* nature of the Buddhist detachment that there lies the weakness and the (at least logical) danger of oriental religions. The Buddhist denies himself in order to kill desire (he does not believe in the value of being). The authentic Christian, also, denies himself, but by *excess of desire* and of faith in the value of being.

This is one of those cases where the same appearances cover contrary realities. It seems to me supremely desirable to unmask the ambiguity here . . . [16]

The biographer Claude Cuénot mentions a further criticism of Teilhard's study whose source he does not disclose, but, judging from the context, it must have come from Monchanin: "Are the religions of India in fact as negative as Teilhard believed?" A new reply came from Teilhard:

Basically, if the religions of India are less negative than I said, that fact does not essentially affect my thesis, the purpose of which is above all to distinguish the two possible essential types of mysticism. It would be quite extraordinary, I confess, for either of these types to be met anywhere in the pure state. I therefore took oriental mysticism as an example, as close as possible, of negativism. Such reservations, or concessions, once made, I still believe that oriental religions and oriental contemplation mean death to action . . . [17]

This passage brings out more clearly than any other that the "road of the West" and the "road of the East" are essentially *two distinct types*. This is a theoretical distinction for the purpose of closer analysis and better understanding. But it does not mean that either of these two types exist pure and unmixed as such in practice or can be found in the individual participant of a particular religious tradition in either West or East. It is important to keep this distinction in mind.

The main ideas found in "The Road of the West" were restated in a lecture given by Teilhard in Paris on January 18, 1933, under the title "*Orient et Occident—la Mystique de la Personnalité.*" We have no published text but only the notes taken down by two listeners. But even these introduce certain fine nuances which may already be a reflection of early criticisms of Teilhard's essay. One listener wrote down, "The opposition between a contemplative Orient and an Occident immersed in life is a questionable one." Another listener continued, "This opposition is not right, not distinct enough; one must show that we carry the virtues of the Orient within us and we may try to bring them to light."[18] Later the notes, when speaking of the East, say with reference to Buddhism:

> Perhaps this *Void* is nothing other but what we call the *Ineffable*, perhaps this is a question of words. But what we can say is that their mysticism does not authorize them towards a positive attitude which makes them seek modern science and western ideas. This gesture by which they try to catch up with us, seems to be condemned by eastern mysticism. Given the conditions of the present world, it is the western conception which tends to become universal.[19]

The term "road of the West" is only used once at the end of the lecture. The short form of the lecture notes helps to highlight perhaps even more than the essay itself the *newness* of what Teilhard calls the "mysticism of convergence." This mysticism is rooted in Christianity because of its central event, the Incarnation, which makes room for the affirmation of the real value of the tangible, material world. However, this spirituality *cannot simply be equated* with the past history of Christian mysticism; it is understood as a new synthesis which transcends the limitation of the past.

## "THE SPIRITUAL CONTRIBUTION OF THE FAR EAST" (1947)

After fifteen years of further reflection, contacts and criticisms, Teilhard wrote the essay "The Spiritual Contribution of the Far East: Some Personal Reflections" in Paris after the war. It is dated February 10, 1947, and, unlike the first essay, it was published during Teilhard's lifetime.[20] Among his numerous writings, this is the only essay which refers to the East in its main title—a reflection of his effort to see things more from an Eastern perspective than before. Meanwhile, he had studied books on China by R. Grousset and perhaps some works by the Indologist O. Lacombe. He had consulted the library of the oriental museum in Paris before writing this essay, which he presents as "personal reflections." It is nevertheless still a very schematic outline, although more succinct than the piece of fifteen years before.

The introduction begins by saying that the world is desperately searching for a soul and that many people look for it as coming in the East. The spirit belongs to the East, matter to the West; this is an easily found assertion in the East.[21] While disclaiming any particular competence in the history of Asiatic thought, Teilhard offers his personal reflections regarding the spiritual contribution that we may rightly await from the Far East.

In the first part he discusses "The Spiritual Modalities of the Far East," of which he distinguishes three. Many Western people simply equate the Eastern mentality with the serenity of the Buddhist, yet one must distinguish the three distinct mentalities of India, China, and Japan. India has an extraordinary sense of the One and the Divine; its basic religious experience is that the invisible is more real than the visible. This sense of the unreality of all phenomena finds its culmination in the Buddhist "intoxication of emptiness."[22] This experience may lead to a pantheistic or theistic attitude, at the opposite of which we find the naturalist and humanist attitude developed by China. Both Taoism and Confucianism kept alive the infallible sense of the primacy of the tangible in relation to the invisible.[23] This sense is even reflected in the transformation which Buddhism underwent in China by substituting the saviour figure of the Bodhisattva Amida for Nirvana. In Japan we find a predominant humanism as well, but it is not so much directed towards the individual as towards the group, which led to the development of a heroic sense of the collective. These three basic attitudes may be presented as a mysticism of God, a mysticism of the individual faced with the world, and a mysticism of the social. At first these three may appear as complementary; on closer examination, however, they show themselves to be exclusive and irreconcilable.

This contention is further discussed in the second part entitled "The Spiritual Formulations of the Far East." What is the specific core of these three basic spiritual currents? While acknowledging the "extreme polymorphism" of Indian thought, which may easily lend itself to fallacious comparisons with Western ideas, Teilhard sees as the very essence of Indian spirituality its particular conception of unity, which must color even any Hindu theism. This unity is achieved through identification with an underlying common ground, an impersonal All, so that the multiple is suppressed or negated, not united, sublimated, and taken up into a higher unity.[24]

Teilhard sees as characteristic of China the taste for the human, the preservation of the harmony of an established order, equilibrium rather than conquest, a wisdom that comes to terms with the world rather than the unique Indian thirst for the transcendent. In Japan, on the contrary, we find movement and a spirit of conquest but no suitable organism to utilize this magnificent force so that it remained enclosed in the narrow boundaries of a race centered on its common origin.

These three religious currents, taken on their own, lead to an exclusive and closed mysticism which cannot provide an answer to all the following problems: God and his transcendence; the world and its value; the individual and the importance of the human person; mankind and social requirements. Although Teilhard recognizes that each of these problems has found particular solutions in the East, no overall synthesis has been attempted. It is the search for this synthesis that he calls the "problem of the spirit" and he thinks that its solution will ultimately only be found in the West.

The third part, "The Road of the West," begins by saying that Europeans are generally not regarded as religious. But underneath the feverish activity of the West a new, original, and powerful, although still badly formulated, mysticism is beginning to take shape. This is basically a *new* solution never tried before. Unity is sought not through negation, but through unification and action. The value of human effort and energy is central here; it is a union through love, through what Teilhard calls elsewhere the "unanimization" of all the elements of the universe. This new mysticism is only emerging now, but it is growing from roots found in the Western tradition. Just as science, after absorbing many ideas and inventions from the East in the past, eventually found its full development and emerged as modern science in the West, Teilhard thinks that a similarly creative religious effort will ultimately come from the West after the transformation of its own religious heritage. Are there not signs that the East is slowly engaging itself "not only technologically but mystically too, with the road of the West?"[25] Such signs of a spiritual rapprochement can be seen in the influence Western thought has had on the foremost contemporary Indian thinkers and on developments in China and Japan.

The last part of the essay is entitled "The Confluence of East and West." This confluence is not understood as a simple coming together of two complementary blocks or the joining of two opposite principles. If a juncture between East and West is to occur, as it will have to one day, the confluence may be likened to the way several rivers suddenly rush forward to use the same opening cut by one of them through a common barrier. For a number of historical reasons, the West has opened up a new path where human consciousness can now develop towards a new stage. The true battle for the spirit is only beginning and all available forces are needed to gain it. In the religious as in the scientific domain, it is only in union with all other people that each individual can hope to attain this goal. The East will not give us a superior form of spirituality, but rather enrich and enlarge the new mystical note that is rising in the West. It is in this contribution that Teilhard sees the indispensable and essential function of the Far East in the realm of spirituality today.

The same theme about two essential types of mysticism is taken up again in a brief note: "A Clarification: Reflections on Two Converse Forms of Spirit" (1950).[26] He distinguishes there between the "spirit of identification," which follows the road of suppression and negation by the elimination of all opposites and the "spirit of unification," which involves tension and centration. In the former, unity is found at the basis, by dissolution; in the latter, unity is reached at the apex, by ultradifferentiation. This note of 1950 has been extensively discussed by R.C. Zaehner in his comparative studies on mysticism[27] and we shall not analyze it here.

A further note of two pages, dated Winter 1951, is entitled "Some Notes on the Mystical Sense: An Attempt at Clarification."[28] In this very brief note the terms "road of the West" and "road of the East" have been almost abandoned. Instead, a more neutral terminology is adopted by presenting a "first path" and a "second path" whose distinguishing feature is the absence or presence of love centered in an *ultra*-personal God. Through its structure and practice, Christianity follows the second path—it *is* this path. This contention is somehow counterbalanced by the assertion that the "path of the West" as a path of unification was born only from the contact of Christianity with the modern world.

The major difficulty in a critical analysis of Teilhard's comparison between Eastern and Western mysticism is his changing vocabulary, with its resulting lack of definition and clarity. He refers to two spiritual currents, two different roads, two "isotypes" of the spirit,[29] and two possible "essential types of mysticism."[30] This sharp distinction between two types of spiritualities is not unlike that which Max Weber drew between "world-rejecting asceticism" and "inner-worldly asceticism." And like Weber's attitude, these spiritualities belong to the category of "ideal types" which must not be confused with contingent historical-empirical realities. This confusion often occurs; it is even more easily made and potentially more dangerous when Teilhard uses terms of geographical limitation such as "the road of the West," where an undertone of superiority might be inferred. This was not his intention, however. Primarily, he was not so much interested in an attitude towards the world which could be classified as either "inner-worldly" or "other-worldly" than in what R. Robertson has called a "*changeful* orientation to the world" in contra-distinction to a "mere" orientation to the world as such.[31] It is here that Teilhard sees a special emphasis in the Western tradition not found elsewhere, its most specific contribution to a synthesis through which it will itself undergo a transformation.

The theme of mysticism is continuous throughout Teilhard's writings. The essays and notes discussed above show that he was preoccupied with the comparison of different kinds of mysticism until the end of his life. He tried to uncover general structures in the mysticism of the past and to inquire how far these mysticisms were either relevant or redundant for a truly contemporary spirituality. Much was found to be redundant and yet, mysticism was for him the very essence of religion and the only spirituality worth pursuing. However, by this he did not mean the traditional, individualistic, soul-searching spirituality often associated with this word. Mysticism is no mere *spirit*-uality, but it is spirit-in-and-through-matter, if one may be allowed this clumsy conjunction. Such a mysticism is directed towards and immersed in the world, both the world of nature and the human world, the social. Such a mysticism leads to interaction, integration, and ultimately convergence. F.C. Happold, in his study on mysticism, has described this as a mysticism of action "springing from the inspiration of a universe seen as moved and com-penetrated by God in the totality of its evolution . . . This is essentially a new type of mysticism, the result of a profound, lifelong, reconciling meditation on religious and scientific truth; and it is thus of immense relevance and significance for a scientific age such as ours."[32]

We still have to answer our initial question: whether Teilhard, in his comparison between Western and Eastern mysticism, shows a certain lack of empathy towards Eastern religions. It is important to know that Teilhard's mystic experience and interpretation were shaped fairly early in his career and were deeply influenced by the important experience of both religion and evolutionary science. His vision of synthesis began to grow during the formative years in Egypt when he first encountered the Orient, and it fully emerged through the even more fundamental experience of life in the trenches during the First World War. He was relatively formed and his basic quest and vision were focused *before* he went to China in 1923. The expedition to the Ordos desert was, however, a third major influence in the making of his spirituality which found expression in his "Mass on the World" written in 1923. But more important, perhaps, than the fact that he went to China as a mature man with a very specific worldview was the relatively closed and semicolonial nature of the scientific, missionary and diplomatic milieu in which he lived for more than twenty years and beyond which he rarely ventured. Both these factors may help to explain a certain narrowness and lack of integration in someone so much concerned with finding a synthesis of views.

As R.C. Zaehner has rightly pointed out in his book *Evolution and Religion,* "although Teilhard had formed his own ideas on Eastern mysticism, he had quite clearly not read even the basic texts in any kind of depth"[33] nor did he have any intimate experience of the monastic and prayer life of Eastern religious traditions. He had discovered Buddhism on his first expedition to China in 1923 and he always seems to have sympathized more with certain aspects of Buddhism than with Hinduism, which he encountered only briefly and rather late. A connoisseur and admirer of Indian spirituality such as Abbé Monchanin could not help criticizing Teilhard's abstract comparison between Eastern and Western mysticism, although basically their judgment coincided in its essentials.[34]

Teilhard later admitted that some of these criticisms were justified and took them into account in the second essay of 1947, although the basic emphasis there, to the disappointment of some of his friends, was still on the "road of the West." It is even more surprising that this essay, although it asserts the supreme Chinese sense of the tangible, of the reality of this world, does not even recognize the relevance and affinity of neo-Confucian organic naturalism or of other parallels in Chinese classical thought to Teilhard's own view of the world.[35] There are also parallels to certain Hindu and Buddhist ideas which reveal themselves to the close observer. But they did not become apparent to Teilhard himself who, despite his efforts to find a synthesis between East and West, nevertheless remained locked in a Western perspective. Born and reared in the West, he spent a major part of his life in the East and seems to be almost the opposite of Sri Aurobindo, the Indian philosopher and mystic, with whom he shares many

similarities in outlook. Yet despite the formative influences of
the West experienced by Aurobindo in his youth, he ultimately
affirms the superiority of his own Eastern tradition, while
Teilhard claims that of the West. To both of them one could
perhaps apply the words of Radhakrishnan: "We are all likely
to consider the defects of another culture as central to that culture
whereas we consider the defects of our own culture as merely
peripheral."[36]

Perhaps this issue is also a question of difference in
generation. At the beginning of the century when Teilhard's and
Aurobindo's views took shape, it was still easier to emphasize
the differences rather than seek the similarities between East and
West. But basically both thinkers were deeply concerned not
with the differences of the past but with the creation of a common
future where the unity of humankind would fully emerge.

C. Cuénot has said, "The Orient meant for Teilhard the
East as opposed to the West and . . . the challenge to effect the
meeting of these two worlds."[37] But this meeting has not been
achieved yet; it remains a task to be attempted. In the realm
of spirituality, both Teilhard's and Aurobindo's positions are to
some extent still isolationist and exclusive of each other. To effect
a true synthesis for the future, a step forward has to be taken.
A much more durable bridge needs to be built which allows
a free exchange between Eastern and Western religious thought
and experience so that elements from one tradition can be
creatively adapted by the other. There are signs that such an
exchange is beginning to grow. As one example among several
of new levels of spiritual inquiry and dialogue, Thomas Merton's
encounter with Buddhist monasticism or the Dalai Lama's interest
in Christian mysticism may be cited. Other, more recent,
examples include the international conferences on Buddhism and
Christianity, and the many interreligious dialogue meetings which
are taking place around the world.

East and West can then no longer be seen as independent
blocks; they must be interpreted in relational terms where one
can be understood only with reference to the other. In the same
way, Eastern and Western mysticism have to be studied in
relationship to each other, not so much in terms of their past,

historical interdependence as in terms of their respective contributions to our present and future religious quest. We must ask, independently of any geographical limitation, what they can offer and contribute to the emergence of a global spirituality. From this perspective, Teilhard de Chardin's comparison between Western and Eastern mysticism may be judged as being somewhere midway between the position of isolation and opposition typical of past approaches, and the position of a fuller rapprochement and integration necessary for the future. The presentation of *types* of mysticism, related to the categories of East and West, is still unsatisfactory and divisive and itself too past-oriented, despite Teilhard's constant attempts to inquire into the necessary conditions for the creation of a future, single-world civilization.

Teilhard's specific contributions to the contemporary understanding of mysticism may be summed up as follows: humankind needs a positive, world-oriented spirituality which can sustain human effort and constructive activity. Such a spirituality alone can help to change and transform not only the resources of the natural world, but ultimately the human community itself. For this task, none of the ancient mysticisms is any longer sufficiently adequate, so that the need for a new path exists today in all religious traditions. As far as Christian spirituality is concerned, it can be seen partly as a derivation of the mysticisms of the East and partly as an orientation which has encouraged *a changeful and dynamic attitude towards the world.* These two tendencies are held in tension, and the history of the Christian tradition indicates an increasing differentiation of these two "roads," which are also found in other religious traditions. Thus the "road of the West" and the "road of the East" must be understood as two dialectical principles whose interaction will eventually lead to a new, higher synthesis termed "a mysticism of convergence." These dialectical principles are not entirely opposed to each other, nor can they be literally equated with either Western or Eastern traditions. In his own usage, Teilhard may have sometimes confused the general, ideal-type function of these principles with their specific, historical-empirical application. However, a deeper knowledge and closer comparison

## 10

## Aurobindo's and Teilhard's Vision
## of the Future of Humankind

The great Indian seer and sage Sri Aurobindo (1872-1950) was deeply concerned about the future of humanity. Reading of Aurobindo's ideal of human unity, one cannot help being reminded of Teilhard de Chardin, who was equally concerned with the future.[1] Today there seems to be an even greater urgency to speak about our future, perhaps more so than when Aurobindo or Teilhard first wrote their works. We realize that we are responsible for our further self-evolution, for planning a better, higher future for all of humankind. This great task cannot be achieved at random, it cannot be left to chance; we have to conceive the future in the present, but where do we find the guidelines for this challenging task? Where do we find an inspiring vision of the future to fire our imagination and heighten our expectation to the utmost? It is here that both Aurobindo's and Teilhard's works are of immense value, presenting as they do, a great vision of the future to our contemporaries.

I am certainly not the first to compare these two great thinkers and point out their similarities. Apart from brief earlier comparisons, Professor R.C. Zaehner devoted an entire book to comparing the two great thinkers, and so did Aurobindo's disciple, K.D. Sethna.[2] The many striking resemblances between

Aurobindo and Teilhard go sometimes even as far as vocabulary and there is certainly a great affinity in their basic concern and intention. Aurobindo's integral philosophy is said to combine both Eastern and Western elements, and Teilhard, who spent many years in the Far East, expressed from his early writings onwards the desire to make East and West meet. Yet Aurobindo and Teilhard never actually met—and if they had done so, one wonders whether they would have understood each other within the limited framework of their own backgrounds—despite all the similarities which we, as later readers, can detect in their basic intuitions.

These two great figures represent some of the best and most essential heritage of their respective religious traditions. Both spent their lives reinterpreting these traditions for the present and the future of humankind. As Professor Zaehner has said, both were obsessed with the theory of evolution. Yet unlike some other evolutionary thinkers, they interpret the ultimate meaning of evolution as being spiritual; evolution is tied to a basic "withinness of things," to use a Teilhardian term, or to the "involution of the spirit in matter," to speak Aurobindo's language. This basic spiritualization of matter, of the whole cosmos, of all life, inspires the readers of both Aurobindo and Teilhard.

Teilhard learned about Aurobindo some time after 1946, when he had returned from China to Paris. The French publisher, Jacques Masui, who had close connections to the Pondicherry Ashram, lent him Aurobindo's masterpiece, *The Life Divine*, which Teilhard acknowledged to be of a similar conception to his own work. According to another source, Teilhard's lifelong friend, Abbé Breuil, wrote to Aurobindo personally about Teilhard in late 1950, pointing out the similarities between the two thinkers. But unfortunately this letter reached the Ashram only after Aurobindo's death in December 1950.[3] Teilhard may have known more than Aurobindo's *The Life Divine*, for in a letter to Lucile Swan, dated March 29, 1951, he wrote, "two weeks ago, somebody sent me the last publication of late Sri Aurobindo."

Jacques Masui assured me that Teilhard's own ideas were becoming known in the Pondicherry Ashram between 1955 and

1957. It is therefore not surprising that comparisons between the two thinkers have been made by Aurobindo's disciples, such as P.B. Saint-Hilaire, K.D. Sethna, and Prema Nandakumar. It is also interesting to note that acquaintance with Teilhard's works can lead people to study Aurobindo's writings—as has been my own case—or vice versa, that earlier acquaintance with Aurobindo can lead subsequently to a study of Teilhard de Chardin, a sequence for which I could also give examples. Aurobindo's and Teilhard's vision of the future is closely linked to their understanding of the previous stages of evolution, the dynamic qualities and directedness of evolution, and the eventual transcending of the present stage of evolution in the future. As I mentioned before, both thinkers understand evolution ultimately in spiritual terms. Evolution is a long, drawn-out process all through time and history, a dialectic of descent and ascent, of involution and evolution; the driving force of evolution is the working-out of the spirit through its infolding and unfolding in matter.

This unfolding of the evolutionary world-spirit right up into the future has been supremely described by Aurobindo in *The Life Divine*. The past stages of evolution have been analyzed in great scientific detail by Teilhard in his book *The Phenomenon of Man*. Here his so-called law of increasing complexity-consciousness and the building-up power of radial energy are discussed. However, Teilhard's thought cannot be linked, as can that of Aurobindo, with one great central work that would give a survey of his entire vision. His writings are more fragmentary, more unfinished; it is often through knowing only *The Phenomenon of Man*, written first and foremost for fellow scientists, that his critics unjustly object to Teilhard's views. To grasp Teilhard's vision, particularly with regard to the future, the essays in *The Future of Man* and other volumes such as *Activation of Energy* have to be taken into account. These present a broader and fuller interpretation of his vision of the future of humankind.

Equipped with the detailed knowledge of modern science, especially paleontology and geology, Teilhard often discusses the unity of humankind in both its origin and destiny. Humankind is one in its biological roots; the rise of consciousness and the rise towards higher forms of consciousness within the evolutionary progress has so far found its summit in the human being. But it has not come to a standstill here: evolution is still on the move, not in terms of a further morphological evolution of the individual human form, but in terms of a further social evolution. If man is the "ascending arrow of evolution," the human powers of reflection and invention, particularly the powers of coreflection at the collective level, are needed to guide, direct, and determine the further self-evolution of humankind.

The future is so important because it is not inevitably given but is made. Thus the future has become a problem—or a great task—for all people. After the great critical steps in the development of evolution, first the advent of life and then the advent of thought, humankind now stands at a third critical threshold: the step into the future which may bring about a higher socialization of humankind, a convergence through the emergence of a collective higher consciousness, a "superconsciousness," a "common soul" of a "superhumanity."

But we are not over the threshold yet. Teilhard was all too conscious of the present evolutionary crisis, the turmoil, disturbance, and general anxiety. He felt that the contemporary existential malaise was perhaps due to the anxiety about the ultimate outcome of the future. How much greater are our anxieties and our anguish today over the deeply disturbing confrontations of power and violence all over the globe. These themes of the critical threshold and the concomitant crises are also very familiar to readers of Sri Aurobindo. Does Aurobindo not speak about the three kinds of revolutions which the world knows, the material, the moral and intellectual, and lastly, the highest, the spiritual?

In *The Life Divine* he writes:

The appearance of human mind and body on the earth marks a crucial step, a decisive change in the course and process of evolution... the being has become awake and aware of himself; there has been made manifest in Mind its will to develop, to grow in knowledge, to deepen the inner and widen the outer existence, to increase the capacities of nature. Man has seen that there can be a higher status of consciousness than his own.[4]

The aim is now the spiritual age of humankind, "a new birth, a new consciousness, an upward evolution of the human being, a descent of the spirit into our members, a spiritual reorganization of our life."[5] But like Teilhard, Aurobindo was aware that this goal has not yet been reached. In the excellent anthology of extracts which P. Saint-Hilaire collected from Aurobindo's writings under the tile *The Future Evolution of Man*, a whole chapter is devoted to the present evolutionary crisis. There the insufficiency of historical religions in providing a solution to our basic problems is discussed. The idea of a world-denying asceticism, not interested in the development of this earth, is denounced too.

Aurobindo writes:

> At present mankind is undergoing an evolutionary crisis in which is concealed a choice of its destiny; for a stage has been reached in which the human mind has achieved in certain directions an enormous development while in others it stands arrested and bewildered and can no longer find its way. A structure of the eternal life has been raised up by man's ever-active mind and life-will, a structure of unmanageable hugeness and complexity . . . Man has created a system of civilization which has become too big for his limited mental capacity and understanding.[6]

How much more true is this today! Teilhard, too, often stressed the enormous powers of contemporary civilization. Because of modern means of communication, the individual has a vastly increased radius of action and society possesses the power both for a further building-up of its structures as well as for its own destruction. The present evolutionary crisis, the manifestations of turmoil and of genesis, of something new being born within humanity, do not give us any concluding evidence for a positive or negative outcome of the future. Humankind's primordial problem today is the problem of survival. Humanity is faced with the grand option, as Teilhard called it, the grand option of building up the earth, or neglecting and rejecting it. Although we cannot know which way humankind will turn, Teilhard himself was carried by a deep-rooted optimism, by an act of hope and faith in the future. It is not only survival that people seek; it is not only to live on and live well; it is to live a qualitatively better, higher life. Humanity seeks a superlife, a superconsciousness.

With equal force Aurobindo stressed that if humanity is to survive, a radical transformation of human nature is indispensable. The past solutions offered by the various religions, as well as the guidance of society by men of spiritual attainment, have proved to be a failure. For Aurobindo "it is only the full emergence of the soul, the full descent of the native light and power of the Spirit and the consequent replacement or transformation and uplifting of our insufficient mental and vital nature by a spiritual and supramental supernature that can effect this evolutionary miracle."[7]

Aurobindo sees many stages in the future evolution of humankind. Beyond the narrow confines of intellectuality, the true spiritual person must be developed. It is in this self-expansion and spiritual growth that the inmost essence of religion — not the outer creeds and institutions — can help: for the inmost essence of religion is for Aurobindo the search for God and the finding of God: the love of God, the delight in God, and lastly, the surrender to God.[8] The soul has to come forward and take the lead of our whole being so that we can open ourselves to infinity, to the external presence, and ascend from a lower to a higher form of consciousness. Aurobindo calls these steps the psychic and spiritual transformation beyond which there lies a third and highest transformation, the descent of the supramental power and its direct action in this world. So it is ultimately the descent of the Supermind, the coming of the divine life upon earth which leads Aurobindo to a vision of the future where both the earth and human beings in their mind and body are utterly transformed and "glorified," if I may use this term.

Thus the central focus of attraction for humanity's further future evolution is the Supermind — *Sacchidananda* — the absolute being, the consciousness and bliss of traditional Hindu philosophy as reinterpreted by Aurobindo's vision of human evolutionary development. For Teilhard the ultimate summit of evolution, in time and beyond time, is the convergence of humankind in Christ Omega, in a fully realized, complete unity and union of love. Omega is the spiritual driving force within evolution and the force of attraction for humanity's evolution from without. To reach Omega, humankind has to strive towards it by further evolving and uniting itself through the forces and energies of love and union. It is in the animating and harnessing of humankind's deepest and most essential energies for this enormous task of building the future, that Teilhard thought the religions of the world, stripped of their legalistic and redundant traits, could make an essential contribution.

Teilhard wrote in *The Future of Man*:

> . . . ahead of, or rather in the heart of, a universe prolonged along its axis of complexity, there exists a divine centre of convergence . . . Let us suppose that from this universal centre, this Omega point, there constantly emanate radiations hitherto only perceptible to those persons whom we call "mystics." Let us further imagine that, as the sensibility of response to mysticism in the human race increases . . . the awareness of Omega becomes so widespread as to warm the earth psychically while physically it is growing cold. Is it not conceivable that mankind, at the end of its totalisation, its folding-in upon itself, may reach a critical level of maturity where, leaving Earth and stars to lapse slowly back into the dwindling mass of primordial energy, it will detach itself from the planet and join the one true, irreversible essence of things, the Omega point.[9]

This hypothesis of a final maturing and ecstasy is for Teilhard the logical conclusion of the increaasing complexity within the material organization and structure of humankind which is accompanied by a concomitant higher form of consciousness. Yet it relates to a future which is beyond the historically given; it is the *eschaton*, the last and final consummation of the human being in God. When one reads Aurobindo's articles written in 1949-50 and published under the title *The Mind of Light*,[10] one may certainly wonder how far his vision of the future is also ultimately an eschatological one. He speaks of man's transformed divine body and the divine life come to earth when man "will live in God and with God, possess God . . ."[11]

If we come back to the more immediate future, we can say that further evolution of humankind can be understood under two aspects: namely, as a further individual or psychological development, and as a further social or collective development. Teilhard's emphasis seems to lie more often on the further social evolution of humankind as a collectivity, on what he calls its "higher socialization." But this higher socialization is at the same time linked, for him, to a deeper personalization because these two aspects are complementary. The higher society which he envisages is centered around the confluence of human thought, which leads to a new collective reality *sui generis*.[12]

Aurobindo seems to be more concerned with the individual and inward aspects, the transformation of a person's inner being. He has charted the map of this inner transformation in Book Two, chapters XXV and XXVI of *The Life Divine*. Here he describes, in deeply moving passages, the journey and stages of the human ascent to the Divine. In comparison, some of Teilhard's writings—with their frequent emphasis on the collective and outward elements of humanity's future—may seem rather less inspiring, less visionary, but these have to be read in connection with other, more mystical passages as found in *The Divine Milieu* and *Writings in Time of War*.

Professor Zaehner has discussed many of the similarities and some of the differences between Sri Aurobindo and Teilhard in his book *Evolution in Religion*. One great difference seems to me that Teilhard envisages the future as a transformation of *humanity as a whole*, while Aurobindo stresses again and again that the *the individual* is the key to the evolutionary movement. The future transformation of people has to occur first and foremost on the individual level, a view which perhaps cannot find support in scientific evidence, as the evolutionary advance seems to be always carried by the group. It is with this stress on the individual that Aurobindo saw the transformation of the future as the work of a few especially endowed individuals, the "gnostic beings," the supermen, who contribute to and bring about the descent of the Supermind.

There are many other aspects in which Sri Aurobindo and Teilhard de Chardin's vision cannot be said to be identical; they are often, however, in the deepest sense of the word, complementary. Aurobindo, in his personal work, experiences, and thought was more concerned with the future individual; Teilhard was concerned first and foremost with the future society. Ultimately, a vision of the future must embrace both aspects.

Today there is a great necessity for accepting complementary viewpoints and achieving a vision of synthesis. Sri Aurobindo and Teilhard de Chardin can both contribute something extremely creative, valuable, and inspiring to the meeting and synthesis of the Eastern and Western traditions, and to a common global vision of the future of humankind. The greatest strength of the two visionaries lies in their bringing people from different backgrounds together and inspiring them in their work and life so that we can build up a better future under the inspiration of a powerful vision full of faith and hope. K.D. Sethna has written about Aurobindo:

> He kindles a vision and initiates a work that bears on the whole human situation . . . Man in every mode and field — the thinker, the scientist, no less than the artist and mystic — man individual and man collective — the modern breaker of ground side by side with the heir of the ages."[13]

Teilhard has said with regard to his own work: "If I have a mission to fulfill, it will only be possible to judge whether I have accomplished it by the extent to which others go beyond me."

Sri Aurobindo and Teilhard de Chardin share a lofty vision of the future of humankind that can still attract and inspire, even though both thinkers died more than thirty years ago and many conditions have changed in the world since then. We may approach their thought more hesitantly and critically today, yet, more than anything else, we need what lies at the heart of their vision: a deep faith in a new birth, in a new consciousness, and in the possibility of a profound spiritual transformation of personal and social life.

*Conclusion*

# Love — The Spirit of One Earth

Love is the free and imaginative outpouring of the spirit over all unexplored paths.

*The Future of Man*

How are we to develop and sustain the powers to bring about a new birth, a new consciousness, and a spiritual transformation of the earth? What efforts are needed to create one human community and build a future together on one earth? In order to live, humans have to choose, especially if they wish to live creatively, imaginatively, hopefully. For this they need inspiration, hope, sustenance — a guiding vision — and the energy to think, act, and work together. Several themes in Teilhard de Chardin's writings can provide such inspiration: the theme of the cosmos and humankind seen together in a tremendous movement of evolution, the rise and transformation of consciousness, the possibility of humankind coming more closely together and developing a common spirit, a sphere of common mind and heart — or what Teilhard called the "noosphere" — leading to greater human unity. He saw many possibilities for such a development, but he also saw that it could only occur if religion was transformed and a new spirituality and mysticism developed, drawing on the religious resources of the entire globe.

One might call this a "mysticism of the real," as it is integrally bound up with loving the real world and working in and through it.

The most powerful energy to transform our world, the energy most needed today, is the spirit of love. Love alone is capable of creating one earth, one human community. Love is *the* spirit of one earth, the life-giving, transforming dynamic at the heart of the noosphere. Teilhard understood this sphere as a thought-love-energy-network, a cosmic web of complex interaction and attraction that weaves new ways of being and sharing. This noospheric vision of Teilhard's — of seeing the globe alive with the transforming powers of love — is a deeply spiritual vision, but concretely rooted in earthly and human realities. To share this vision one must enter deeply into his life and thought. Then one discovers how love, similar to the other great themes of his work, is deeply rooted in the experiences and personal encounters of his life. Given the absolute centrality of love in his life and cosmic vision, it is surprising that no major study of Teilhard's thought has been devoted to this subject.

The theme of love appears in his earliest writings, the *Writings in Time of War*, and recurs again and again through most of his essays until it is emphatically highlighted in the late autobiographical essays "The Heart of Matter" (1950) and "The Christic" (1955). Like a musician, Teilhard develops the theme of love in a succession of variations set to different occasions and contexts. To fully explore the richness and depth of this theme, one would have to not only trace his thoughts, but connect them to his relationships and root them in their experiential matrix. This cannot be done here, but let us conclude with some remarks on Teilhard's understanding of love.

As with other phenomena in the world, Teilhard wished to trace the evolution of love. To begin with, he saw love as a cosmic energy, a universal form of attraction linked to the inwardness of things. More recently this has been poetically described as allurement in Brian Swimme's cosmic creation story, *The Universe Is A Green Dragon*.[1] In a general sense love is the most universal, the most powerful, the most mysterious of cosmic energies linked to primordial creativity and enchantment. For

Teilhard love is also central to the understanding of personalization and socialization. He wrote a great deal on both the love of the world and the love of God but saw it as his particular task to integrate and thereby transform the two into one sense of fullness and plenitude. He spoke of the spiritualization of love, whereby lovers converge in a divine center, thereby creating a love that is both universal and personal. The notion of a higher "superlove" is linked to Teilhard's idea of a "supercenter" of cosmic and human evolution, the supreme pole Christ Omega. The idea of a kind of "superlove" is also connected to the specific form of Christian love, the love of one's neighbor expressed through charity and compassionate concern for other people's well-being. Teilhard wrote some moving passages on the phenomenon of Christian love, which he described as "a specifically new state of consciousness,"[2] for he considered the dynamic of love as one of the most distinctive elements of Christianity.

Elsewhere, however, he also writes very realistically about the difficulties of love, the complexities of human relations and personal attraction, the unsettling distraction which the encounter with another person, at times simply called "the Other," can bring into one's life. Teilhard once described the "pains of personalization" as the pains of plurality, the pain of differentiation, and the pain of metamorphosis. In the essay "Sketch of a Personalistic Universe" (1936), he says, "The physical structure of the universe is love" and that the manifestation of this fundamental power reveals itself "to our consciousness in three successive stages: in woman (for man), in society, in the All — by the sense of sex, of humanity and of the cosmos."[3] Sexuality, the sense of humanity, and the cosmic sense are thus closely interwoven in Teilhard's reflections on the phenomenon of love.

To understand the richness and complexity of Teilhard's ideas on love, their personal, experiential source, one would have to trace the place of love and friendship in his life. The emergence of his literary and philosophical activity was, in his early years, as is well known, greatly helped and enhanced by a deep personal relationship to his cousin Marguerite, although this has found little explicit reference in his essays. But one can recognize it indirectly in certain remarks, such as those found in "The Mystical Milieu" (1917), where he speaks about being initiated through "three things, tiny, fugitive: a song, a sunbeam, a glance." Particular experiences led him to a larger vision of God and the universe:

> Through the sharp tips of the three arrows which had pierced me the world itself had invaded my being. . . And, under the glance that fell upon me, the shell in which my heart slumbered, burst open. With pure and generous love, a new energy penetrated into me – or emerged from me, which, I cannot say – that made me feel that I was as vast and as loaded with richness as the universe . . . Lord, it is you who, through the imperceptible goadings of sense-beauty, penetrated my heart in order to make its life flow out into yourself. You came down into me by means of a tiny scrap of created reality; and then, suddenly, you unfurled your immensity before my eyes, and displayed yourself to me as a Universal Being.[4]

Pure and generous love as a new energy that grows to cosmic proportions – this theme recurs again and again. In October 1926 Teilhard wrote to his friend Leóntine Zanta: "I sometimes get vague and undefined longings to gather a small group of friends around me and – through all the admitted conventions – give the example of a life in which nothing would count but the preoccupation with, and love for, *all* the earth. What I'm saying must sound very pagan, and far below the example of pure detachment formerly given by St. Francis."[5]

Teilhard was a beloved and precious friend to many, as can be seen from his published letters, including those to several women friends. Like many before him, he sang the praises of the powers of love, which deepen our development as a person and are equally necessary for a fuller, richer development of human society as a community, a genuine option available to us now:

> All that matters at this crucial moment is that the massing together of individualities should not take the form of a functional and enforced mechanisation of human energies (the totalitarian principle),

but of a "conspiracy" informed by love. Love has always been carefully eliminated from realist and positivist concepts of the world; but sooner or later we shall have to acknowledge that it is the fundamental impulse of Life, or, if you prefer, the one natural medium in which the rising course of evolution can proceed. With love omitted there is truly nothing ahead of us except the forbidding prospect of standardisation and enslavement – the doom of ants and termites. It is through love and within love that we must look for the deepening of our deepest self, in the life-giving coming together of humankind. Love is the free and imaginative outpouring of the spirit over all unexplored paths. It links those who love in bonds that unite but do not confound, causing them to discover in their mutual contact an exaltation capable, incomparably more than any arrogance of solitude, of arousing in the heart of their being all that they possess of uniqueness and creative power.[6]

Rooted in matter, love is an all-transforming spiritual energy. According to Teilhard, we must summon and harness its power as we have harnessed the powers of wind and water, of atoms and genes, in order to build a future worth living which will extend rather than diminish our capacity of being human. In his essay "The Spirit of the Earth" (1931), he describes love as one of the essential components in the "sense of the earth," "the most universal, the most tremendous, and the most mysterious of the cosmic forces." He briefly explains what he means by this:

In its most primitive forms, when life was scarcely individualized, love is hard to distinguish from molecular forces; one might think of it as a matter of chemisms or tactisms. Then little by little it becomes distinct, though still *confused* for a very long time with the simple function of reproduction. Not till hominization does it at last reveal the secret and manifold virtues of its violence. "Hominized" love is distinct from all other love, because the "spectrum" of its warm and penetrating light is marvellously enriched. No longer only a unique and periodic attraction for purposes of material fertility; but an unbounded and continuous possibility of contact between minds rather than bodies; the play of countless subtle antennae seeking one another in the light and darkness of the soul; the pull towards mutual sensibililty and completion, in which preoccupation with preserving the species gradually dissolves in the greater intoxication of two people creating a world.

And he goes on to say:

> It is fact that through woman the universe advances towards man
> . . . If only man would turn and see the reality of the universe
> shining in the spirit and through the flesh . . . Woman stands before
> him as the lure and symbol of the world. He cannot embrace her
> except by himself growing, in his turn, to a world scale. And because
> the world is always growing and always unfinished and always ahead
> of us, to achieve his love man is engaged in a limitless conquest
> of the universe and himself. In this sense, man can only attain
> woman by consummating a union with the universe. Love is a sacred
> reserve of energy; it is like the blood of spiritual evolution.[7]

One could compare these remarks with similar ones on the
relationship between the sexes elsewhere. Reflecting on "the sense
of humanity," Teilhard writes: "By the love of man and woman
a thread is wound that stretches to the heart of the world."[8]
There no doubt exists a personal dimension to this insight, as
is evident from "The Heart of Matter" (1950), which Teilhard
once described as "a sort of history of my spiritual adventure."
Speaking there of "The Feminine, or the Unitive," he says that
the story of his inner vision would leave out an essential element
if he did not mention that from the critical moment when he
rejected many of the molds in which his family life and religion
had formed him and began to express himself in terms really
his own, he had experienced no further self-development without
some feminine influence at work.

With its rootedness in life, Teilhard's vision of love as
transforming energy is a powerful one, without being wholly
satisfactory in the light of contemporary experience. In some
passages he called the unitive element that is love — covering
such diverse meanings as interatomic attraction, cosmic creativity,
human sexual love, sacrificial love, and the love of God — "the
eternal feminine," an expression he was fond of in his early
writings. In fact, he devoted an entire essay to this theme, which
has been extensively commented upon by Henri de Lubac.[9]
Teilhard tried to elucidate the meaning of human sexual
differentiation and the mutual attraction between the sexes for
the understanding and practice of spirituality. Unfortunately,

however, his treatment and even more de Lubac's commentary on "The Eternal Feminine" (1918) often fall far short of the very integration they seek. They invite a thoroughgoing critique which still needs to be undertaken. The "feminine" as a principle of unification and love is here sometimes imperceptibly and uncritically equated with "woman" as an actual sexual being while the concrete attitude to and expectations about woman's image and roles are still to a large extent determined by traditional ascetic theology and its male celibate representatives. In spite of his universalism and search for integration, Teilhard's understanding of the "feminine" remains locked in an almost exclusively male-centered perspective. Here again, contemporary experience, especially as reflected in the feminist movement, has gone further in its search for an integral spirituality and a new understanding of love.

This criticism is of a particular element in the intellectual expression and construction of Teilhard's vision, not of the fundamental thrust and dynamic of the vision as a whole. He also wrote in "The Heart of Matter":

> However primordial in human psychism the plenifying encounter of the sexes may be, and however essential to its structure, there is nothing to prove (indeed, the opposite is much more true) that we yet have an exact idea of the functioning of this fundamental complementarity or of the best forms in which it can be effected. We have a marriage that is always polarized, socially, towards reproduction, and a religious perfection that is always represented, theologically, in terms of separation: and there can be no doubt that we lack a third road between the two. I do not mean a *middle* road, but a higher, a road that is *demanded* by the revolutionary transformation that has recently been effected in our thought by the transposition of the notion of "spirit." For the spirit that comes from dematerialization, we have seen, we have substituted the spirit that comes from synthesis.[10]

He then goes on to speak about his understanding of "noogenesis," the cosmic birth and rebound of thought, which now needs to be complemented by what he calls "the break-through in amorization," the transformation of the world through the powers of love.

For Teilhard love, divine and human, was *the* inexhaustible source of energy, a power of unification and transformation that creates all worlds, whether cosmic, social, or personal, and without which we cannot create the new world we need at our present critical stage in history. He used the rich texture of his experience together with his visionary mind's ability for analysis and synthesis to praise the powers of love — a theme running through his entire work, as love is linked to the emergence of consciousness, the growth of personality, to cosmic, human, and social evolution, to creative union, the full flowering of the noosphere, and to the mystical love of God. Love was for Teilhard the thread to the heart of the universe and to the heart of God, a thread he wove together by the powers of his intellectual insight and the depth and warmth of his feeling. He himself was a person filled with love — with love for the world and its development (he wrote *The Divine Milieu* "for those who love the world"), with love for his church and order, and most of all, with love for "the ever greater Christ." He also gave a very special place to the power of Christian love in the scheme of human evolution, as seen in this passage from the end of *The Phenomenon of Man*:

Christian love is incomprehensible to those who have not experienced it. That the infinite and the intangible can be lovable, or that the human heart can beat with genuine charity for a fellow-being, seems impossible to many people I know — in fact almost monstrous. But whether it be founded on an illusion or not, how can we doubt that such a sentiment exists, and even in great intensity? We have only to note crudely the results it produces unceasingly all around us. Is it not a positive fact that thousands of mystics, for twenty centuries, have drawn from its flame a passionate fervour that outstrips by far in brightness and purity the urge and devotion of any human love? . . . is it not a fact . . . that if the love of God were extinguished in the souls of the faithful, the enormous edifice of rites, of hierarchy and of doctrines that comprises the Church would instantly revert to the dust from which it rose? It is a phenomenon of capital importance for the science of man that, over an appreciable region of the earth, a zone of thought has appeared and grown in which a genuine universal love has not only been conceived and preached, but has also been shown to be psychologically possible and operative in practice. It is all the more capital inasmuch as, far from decreasing, the movement seems to wish to gain still greater speed and intensity.[11]

If one generalizes what Teilhard wrote about the place of love within human evolution, one can say that the phenomenon of religion, spirituality, and mysticism is central to the development of humankind and presents a progressive interiorization and centration dependent on the unifying powers of the phenomenon of love. Teilhard likened its power to the power of fire. The symbol of fire, so frequent in his writings, stands for the warmth and radiance of love and light as well as for the fusion and transformation of the elements. Fire can both transform and destroy. The fire of love may be the only energy capable of extinguishing the threat of another fire — that of universal conflagration and destruction.

For the spirit of one earth to emerge, we have to foster planetary consciousness and a global outlook. Our need for human transformation and spiritual evolution is great and urgent. Many are seeking a new spirit to bring about the unity of our knowledge and experience, of science and religion in order to ensure the future of the earth and humankind. Through blending the insights of science, rationality, love, and mysticism, Teilhard de Chardin has much to give to our time where these aspects are still kept apart to our peril.[12] His noosphere is a sphere of both knowledge and love, his mysticism a mysticism of knowing and loving. Thus one can describe his spirituality as empowered by the all-transforming dynamic of love that radiates through all creation and sets the noosphere aflame.

Using an analogy from music, as Teilhard sometimes did when he referred to "hearing the fundamental harmony of the universe," one could say that his entire work is an immense symphony of love with numerous variations in major and minor keys, many of which still remain to be decoded. Yet all over the world there exist individuals who have been inspired by Teilhard's vision and have applied his insights in their own lives and work. They have experienced what Robert Muller has called

"Teilhardian enlightenments,"[13] which include the awareness of the global dimensions of humanity and the urgent need for spiritual transformation.

There are other writers on global spirituality today, besides Teilhard de Chardin, but few see with such clarity and speak with such power on the human ascent to the spirit wedded to the cosmic sense of the earth and the global sense of humanity. The vision of "the free and imaginative outpouring of the spirit over all unexplored paths" makes us envisage the common future of one earth created by the powers of love.

# Notes

*Introduction*

1. Scottish Churches Council Working Party Report on "Spirituality," (Dunblane: Scottish Churches House, 1977), p. 3.

2. See the essays in Robert Muller, *New Genesis — Shaping A Global Spirituality* (New York: Doubleday, 1982).

3. See the essays in P. Teilhard de Chardin, *Writings in Time of War* (London: Collins, 1968). Teilhard's inner struggle in arriving at a harmonious balance and synthesis of his affective and intellectual life by experiencing cosmic life and consciousness as signs of an all-pervading divine presence is analyzed by Richard Brüchsel, "The Meaning of the 'Sense of Plenitude' in Teilhard de Chardin's Early Life and Work — An Interpretation," M.A. dissertation, University of Leeds, 1987.

4. See the essay "The Christic" in P. Teilhard de Chardin, *The Heart of Matter* (London: Collins, 1978), pp. 80-102.

5. See René d'Ouince, *Un prophète en procès* (Paris: Aubier Montaigne), 1970, 2 vols.

6. In P. Teilhard de Chardin, *Human Energy* (London: Collins, 1969), pp. 19-47.

7. Ibid., p. 37 f.

8. See M.D. Bryant, J. Maniatis, and T. Hendricks, eds., *Assembly of World Religions 1985. Spiritual Unity and the Future of the Earth* (New York: Paragon House, 1986).

9. London: SPCK, 1986.

10. Published by The Crossroad Publishing Company, New York, 1985 and Routledge & Kegan Paul, London, 1986.

11. See Bernard McGinn, John Meyendorff, and Jean Leclercq, eds., *Christian Spirituality – Origins to the Twelfth Century* (London: Routledge & Kegan Paul, 1986), p. xiv.

12. Teilhard's ideas are compared with Indian thought in Beatrice Bruteau, *Evolution toward Divinity: Teilhard de Chardin and the Hindu Traditions* (Wheaton, Ill.: The Theosophical Publishing House, 1974), with Chinese thought in Marie-Ina Bergeron, *La Chine et Teilhard* (Paris: Jean Pierre Delarge, 1976). For a general comparison with Eastern thought, especially with regard to mysticism, see Ursula King *Towards a New Mysticism: Teilhard de Chardin and Eastern Religions* (London: Collins and New York: Seabury Press, 1980). A recent study of Teilhard and Taoist thought in relationship to contemporary Western thinking, looking especially at ideas on unity and distinction, aspects of change, and human values is Allerd Stikker, "A Comparison of Some Major Aspects of Western Thought, Taoist Philosophy and Teilhard de Chardin," M.A. dissertation, University of Leeds, 1986. See also Allerd Stikker, *Tao, Teilhard en westers denken* (Amsterdam: Bres, 1986).

*Chapter 1*

1. In P. Teilhard de Chardin, *Human Energy* (London: Collins, 1969), pp. 163-81.

2. In P. Teilhard de Chardin, *The Heart of Matter* (London: Collins, 1978), pp. 14-79.

3. Ibid., pp. 75-76.

4. In P. Teilhard de Chardin, *Toward the Future* (London: Collins, 1975), pp. 163-208.

5. See Charles E. Raven, *Teilhard de Chardin, Scientist and Seer* (London: Collins and New York: Harper and Row, 1962).

6. See *Human Energy*, p. 165.

7. New York: Doubleday, 1982.

8. P. Teilhard de Chardin, *Science and Christ* (London: Collins, 1968), p. 203.

9. See chapters 7 and 8 in this book. A detailed discussion of Teilhard's mysticism and his attitude towards Eastern religions is found in my book *Towards a New Mysticism: Teilhard de Chardin and Eastern Religions* (London: Collins and New York: Seabury Press, 1980).

10. See *Human Energy*, p. 163.

11. Mary and Ellen Lukas, *Teilhard: A Biography* (London: Collins, 1977).

*Chapter 2*

1. *International Encyclopedia of Social Sciences* (New York: The Macmillan Company and The Free Press, 1968), vol. 14, p. 545.

2. P. Teilhard de Chardin, *The Phenomenon of Man* (London: Collins, 1966), pp. 278-79.

3. The distinction between the words *survival* and *superlife* is perhaps more adequately expressed by the original French terms *survie* and *survivance*.

4. The implications of this idea have been worked out by F.G. Elliott in "The Origin of Life and the World Vision of Teilhard de Chardin: The Creative Aspect of Evolution" in C. Cuénot, F.G. Elliott, et al., *Evolution, Marxism and Christianity – Studies in the Teilhardian Synthesis* (London: Garnstone Press, 1967), pp. 11-29.

5. *The Phenomenon of Man*, p. 305; see the entire postscript on "The Essence of The Phenomenon of Man" (pp. 300-310), especially subsection 3 on "The Social Phenomenon or the Ascent towards a Collective Threshold of Reflection."

6. *The Phenomenon of Man*, p. 248.

7. P. Teilhard de Chardin, *The Future of Man* (London: Collins, 1965), p. 137; see the whole essay on "A Great Event Foreshadowed: The Planetisation of Mankind," written in December 1945. It speaks of "Mankind in the Re-shaping."

8. Buckminster Fuller, "Planetary Planning," Jawaharlal Nehru Memorial Lecture, New Delhi, November 13, 1969, pp. 6 and 24.

9. *The Future of Man*, p. 126; the subtitle reads "An Irresistible Physical Process: The Collectivisation of Mankind."

10. This criticism was made by Teilhard's friend François Russo in "La Socialisation selon Teilhard," *Revue de l'Action Populaire*, December, 1962, p. 1153.

11. Roger Garaudy, "The Meaning of Life and History in Marx and Teilhard de Chardin: Teilhard's Contribution to the Dialogue between Christians and Marxists" in C. Cuénot, F.G. Elliott, et al, *Evolution*, pp. 58-72 (see note 4 above).

12. *The Phenomenon of Man*, p. 308, note 2 says: "For a Christian believer it is interesting to note that the final success of hominisation (and thus cosmic involution) is positively guaranteed by the 'redeeming virtue' of the God incarnate in his creation. But this takes us beyond the plan of phenomenology."

13. *The Future of Man*, p. 234.

14. Quoted in C. Cuénot, *Teilhard de Chardin – A Biographical Study* (London: Burns and Oates, 1965), p. 358.

*Chapter 3*

1. P. Teilhard de Chardin, *Toward the Future* (London: Collins, 1975), p. 124.

2. P. Teilhard de Chardin, *The Phenomenon of Man* (London: Collins, 1966), p. 265.

3. Adam Curle, *Education for Liberation* (London: Tavistock Publications, 1973).

4. Ibid., p. 32.

5. E.F. Schumacher, "The End of an Era," in *The Soil Association*, vol. 1, no. 1, September, 1975.

6. Joseph Needham, *Within the Four Seas: The Dialogue of East and West* (London: George Allen and Unwin, 1969), p. 26.

*Chapter 4*

1. Dorothy Emmet, "Editorial," in *Theoria to Theory*, vol. 14, no. 4, 1981, p. 269.

2. See H. de Lubac, *The Religion of Teilhard de Chardin* (London: Collins, 1967); T. Corbishley, *The Spirituality of Teilhard de Chardin (London: Fontana,* 1971; R. Faricy, *All Things in Christ – Teilhard de Chardin's Spirituality* (London: Fount Paperbacks, 1981); and *Christian Faith and my Everyday Life – The Spiritual Doctrine of Teilhard de Chardin* (Middlegreen/Slough: St. Paul's Publications, 1981).

3. Discussed in detail in J. Lyons' *The Cosmic Christ in Origen and Teilhard de Chardin: A Comparative Study* (Oxford: Oxford University Press, 1982), where seeds for a possible new christology are brought together.

4. For a fuller treatment of Teilhard's understanding of different mysticisms, see U. King, *Towards A New Mysticism – Teilhard de Chardin and Eastern Religions* (London: Collins and New York: Seabury Press, 1980). The *via tertia* is discussed on pp. 200-204.

5. Except for Corbishley, *The Spirituality of Teilhard de Chardin*, pp. 7-16.

6. J. Moore, *Sexuality/Spirituality – A Study of Feminine/Masculine Relationship* (Tisbury/Wiltshire: Element Books, 1980), provides an example of this where he writes: "Spiritual evolution is essentially and uniquely an individual responsibility. No group can of itself evolve, only individual members within it can do so" (p. 225). One could also quote examples from the Indian tradition.

7. See E.H. Cousins, "Teilhard de Chardin and the Religious Phenomenon" (paper presented at the International UNESCO Symposium on the Occasion of the Centenary of the Birth of Teilhard de Chardin), Paris, September 16-18, 1981.

8. See the detailed study by R.E. Whitson, *The Coming Convergence of World Religions* (New York: Newman Press, 1971). The issue is also discussed by E.H. Cousins (see note 7) and W. Cantwell Smith, *Towards A World Theology: Faith and the Comparative History of Religion* (London: Macmillan, 1981).

9. E.H. Cousins, "Teilhard de Chardin and The Religious Phenomenon," pp. 9-10.

10. In another cultural and religious context, Sri Aurobindo has looked for such integration in his "integral yoga." So far comparisons have mainly been undertaken in short articles. R.C. Zaehner's *Evolution in Religion – A Study in Sri Aurobindo and Pierre Teilhard de Chardin* (Oxford: Clarendon Press, 1971) remains superficial and sketchy. A thorough critique of this work, although not satisfactory either, has been undertaken by one of Sri Aurobindo's close disciples, K.D. Sethna, *The Spirituality of the Future – A Search Apropos R.C. Zaehner's Study in Sri Aurobindo and Teilhard de Chardin* (London and Toronto: Associated University Presses, 1981). See also Chapter 10 in this book, "Aurobindo's and Teilhard's Vision of the Future of Humankind."

11. P. Teilhard de Chardin, *Writings in Time of War* (London: Collins, 1968), p. 144.

12.  T.M. King, *Teilhard's Mysticism of Knowing* (New York: Seabury Press, 1981).

13.  For the great outlines of this theme see R. Muller's inspiring book *New Genesis: Shaping a Global Spirituality* (New York: Doubleday, 1982).

*Chapter 5*

1.  Patrick Grant, *Literature of Mysticism in Western Tradition* (London: Macmillan, 1983), p. 14.

2.  Ursula King, "Current Perspectives in the Study of Mysticism," in *Studies in Mystical Literature*, February 1, 1982, pp. 1-17.

3.  London: Sheldon Press.

4.  Oxford: Oxford University Press.

5.  See the essay "My Fundamental Vision" (1948) in P. Teilhard de Chardin, *Toward the Future* (London: Collins, 1975), pp. 163-208.

6.  This important essay is included in a book of the same title; see P. Teilhard de Chardin, *The Heart of Matter* (London: Collins, 1978), pp. 13-79.

7.  In *The Heart of the Matter*, pp. 80-102.

8.  Originally published in P. Teilhard de Chardin, *Ecrits du Temps de la Guerre* (Paris: Grasset, 1965), pp. 263-79, it remained untranslated until it was included as "My Universe" in *The Heart of the Matter*, pp. 196-208.

9.  P. Teilhard de Chardin, *Journal 26 août – 4 janvier 1919* (Paris: Fayard, 1975), p. 223; my translation.

10.  London: Collins, 1968.

11.  This has been studied in detail by C.F. Mooney, *Teilhard de Chardin and the Mystery of Christ* (London: Collins, 1966) and J.A. Lyons, *The Cosmic Christ in Origen and Teilhard de Chardin* (Oxford: Oxford University Press, 1982).

12.  P. Teilhard de Chardin, *Christianity and Evolution* (London: Collins, 1971), p. 171. Teilhard also spoke of "pan-Christism," a term taken over from Maurice Blondel; see H. de Lubac, ed., *Blondel et Teilhard de Chardin, correspondance commentée* (Paris: Beauchesne, 1965), p. 52 f.

13.  *The Heart of the Matter*, p. 47.

14.  See *The Heart of the Matter*, p. 153; my translation.

15.  P. Teilhard de Chardin, *Letters to Two Friends, 1926-1952* (London: Fontana, 1972), p. 59.

16.  *Christianity and Evolution*, p. 68.

17.  Ibid., p. 102.

18.  *Toward the Future*, pp. 209-11.

19.  Teilhard sees love in dynamic, evolutionary terms and has many passages about the changing character of love, its "evolution." This is discussed in more detail in the Conclusion of this book.

20.  *Toward the Future*, p. 210.

21.  Ibid., p. 211.

22.  The diagram in this form is my own, but it is adapted from a similar one in P. Teilhard de Chardin, *The Future of Man* (London: Collins, 1965), p. 269.

23. *Writings in Time of War*, p. 14.

24. For more details, see chapter 8 on "Teilhard's Association with the World Congress of Faiths" in this book. The quotation is taken from an unpublished duplicated report of the 1948 conference of the *Union des Croyants*, Paris; the translation is mine.

25. *Christianity and Evolution*, p. 93.

26. In P. Leroy, ed., *Lettres familières de Pierre Teilhard de Chardin mon ami 1948-1955* (Paris: Editions du Centurion, 1976), p. 193; my translation.

27. P. Teilhard de Chardin, *Science and Christ* (London: Collins, 1968), p. 112.

28. Teilhard found this expression, which he was fond of quoting, in J.V.L. Casserley, *The Retreat of Christianity in the Modern World* (London: Longmans, 1952).

29. See H. de Lubac, ed., *Lettres Intimes à Auguste Valensin, Bruno de Solages, Henri de Lubac, André Ravier 1919-1955* (Paris: Editions Aubier-Montaigne, second edition, 1974), pp. 450 and 460.

30. See the subtitle in P. Teilhard de Chardin, *Activation of Energy* (London: Collins, 1970), p. 226.

31. Ibid., p. 227.

32. Based on notes found in Teilhard's unpublished *Carnet de Lecture*.

33. See especially Teilhard's essay "The Spiritual Contribution of the Far East" in *Toward the Future*, pp. 134-47. This is discussed in more detail in chapter 9, "Teilhard's Comparison of Western and Eastern Mysticism" in this book.

34. These are discussed in the chapter "Exploring Convergence: The Contribution of World Faiths."

35. Mentioned in P. Teilhard de Chardin, *The Phenomenon of Man* (London: Collins, 1966), p. 283, this idea is often discussed in letters and notes of his last years.

36. See ibid., pp. 283-85.

37. *Lettres familières*, p. 188.

38. See ibid., p. 193 for a detailed discussion of the role of a rightly understood "energetics."

39. See Teilhard's letter to E. Mounier in *Science and Christ*, pp. 221-23.

40. *Toward the Future*, p. 105.

41. P. Teilhard de Chardin, *Human Energy* (London: Collins, 1969), p. 110.

42. Ibid., p. 112.

43. F.C. Happold, *Mysticism: A Study and Anthology* (London: Penguin Books, 1981), pp. 394-395.

44. London: SPCK.

45. See A. Curle, *Mystics and Militants: A Study of Awareness, Identity, and Social Action* (London: Tavistock, 1972).

46. A.J. Deikman, *The Observing Self: Mysticism and Psychotherapy* (Boston: Beacon Press, 1982).

47. W. Cantwell Smith, *Towards a World Theology: Faith and the Comparative History of Religion* (London: Macmillan, 1981), p. 147.

*Chapter 6*

1. These two basic tendencies of Teilhard's mind, his "cosmic" and "christic" sense, have been admirably analyzed by C.F. Mooney in *Teilhard de Chardin and the Mystery of Christ* (London: Collins, 1966, ch. 1).

2. R.C. Zaehner, *The Convergent Spirit* (London: Routledge and Kegan Paul, 1963), p. 16.

3. H. de Lubac has given such an interpretation in *The Religion of Teilhard de Chardin* (London: Collins, 1967).

4. P. Teilhard de Chardin, *The Future of Man* (London: Collins, 1965); idem, *The Science of Christ* (London: Collins, 1968).

5. *Science of Christ*, p. 99.

6. Ibid.

7. *Future of Man*, p. 189.

8. Ibid., p. 186 f.

9. *Science of Christ*, p. 102.

10. *Future of Man*, p. 261 f.

11. Ibid., pp. 260 and 268.

12. *Science of Christ*, p. 121.

13. P. Teilhard de Chardin, *The Activation of Energy* (London: Collins, 1970), p. 239 f., partly my translation.

14. *Future of Man*, p. 266 f.

15. *Science of Christ*, pp. 113-17.

16. *Activation of Energy*, p. 240.

17. *Science of Christ*, p. 120.

18. Ibid, p. 144.

19. *Future of Man*, p. 76; partly my translation.

20. Ibid., p. 78 f.

21. *Science of Christ*, p. 204.

22. *Future of Man*, p. 263.

23. Ibid., p. 224.

24. See the essay of this title in *Future of Man*, pp. 37-60.

25. *Future of Man*, p. 188.

26. Ibid., pp. 187, 88.

27. Ibid., p. 120.

28. *Science of Christ*, p. 190.

29. Ibid., p. 191.

30. *Future of Man*, p. 92.

31. *Science of Christ*, p. 164.

32. Ibid., p. 54; partly my translation. A detailed analysis of the christological interpretation of the point Omega can be found in C.F. Mooney, *Mystery of Christ*.

33. *Future of Man*, pp. 80, 81.

34. *Activation of Energy*, p. 238.

35. Ibid., p. 242; partly my translation.

36. *Science of Christ*, p. 127.

37. Ibid., p. 126.

38. Ibid., p. 124.

39. Ibid,, p. 104.

40. *Activation of Energy*, p. 48.

41. *Science of Christ*, pp. 163, 164, 170.

42. *Activation of Energy*, p. 242; partly my translation.

43. R.C. Zaehner, *Convergent Spirit*, p. 16.

44. For this distinction, see R.W. Hepburn, "Mysticism, Nature and Assessment of" in *The Encyclopedia of Philosophy* (New York: The Macmillan Co. and The Free Press, 1967), vol. 5, p. 429.

45. *Activation of Energy*, p. 383.

## Chapter 7

1. The text of this chapter was originally delivered in London as the third Francis Younghusband Lecture and later published in *World Faiths* (no. 106, Autumn 1978), the journal of the World Congress of Faiths.

2. R.E. Whitson, *The Coming Convergence of World Religions* (New York: Newman Press, 1971).

3. Ibid., p. 52.

4. W. Johnston, *The Inner Eye of Love* (London: Collins, 1978), p. 69.

5. Quoted in J. Waardenburg, *Classical Approaches to the Study of Religion* (The Hague, Paris, New York: Mouton, 1973), p. 666.

6. R.E. Whitson, *Convergence*, pp. 185, 187.

## Chapter 8

1. Quoted from the aims of the World Congress of Faiths as stated in their journal, *World Faiths*. The information about the development of the French branch is taken from a cyclostyled historical survey entitled *Le Congrès Universel des Croyants — Historique — 1946-1962*.

2. His description of the early years of the French branch and Teilhard's association with it can be found in J. Bacot, "Autour du Congrès Universel des Croyants: Quelques Evocations," in *Cahiers P.T.de Chardin 2* (Paris: Seuil, 1960), pp. 143-49.

3. Madame Lemaître was for many years the secretary of the *Amis de l'Orient* at the *Musée Guimet*, where up to 1958 the meetings of the French branch of the World Congress of Faiths took place. Before the foundation of the French branch in 1947, she had already published her first book *Le mystere de la mort dans les religions de l'Asie* (Paris: Presses Universitaires, 1943). Later she became particularly known through the publication of her two-volume anthology, *Textes mystiques d'Orient et d'Occident* (Paris: Plon, 1955). She refers to this work several times in her correspondence with Teilhard. Her other publications include *Ramakrishna* (Paris: Seuil, 1954), and *Hindouisme ou*

Sanatana Dharma (Paris: Fayard, 1957), later translated into English. For information about her, see Marcelle Auclair, *A la Grâce de Dieu* (Paris: Seuil, 1973), pp. 95-103. Solange Lemaître left a short account of her friendship with Teilhard: "Le Père Teilhard de Chardin – Sa Présence," now published in *Cahiers P.T. de Chardin 2* (Paris: Seuil, 1960), pp. 151-57.

4. Cf. Claude Cuénot, *Teilhard de Chardin – A Biographical Study* (London: Burns and Oates, 1965). It was during their regular philosophical discussions that in 1925 Teilhard first coined his important term *noosphere*, which was adopted by E. Le Roy for his own writings. Cf. Cuénot, *Teilhard de Chardin*, p. 57 f.

5. C. Cuénot, *Teilhard de Chardin*, p. 296.

6. J. Bacot, "Quelques Evocations," p. 146.

7. Madame B. d'Hauteville in a personal communication to the author. Teilhard's place on the committee was later, after his death, given to his fellow Jesuit and close collaborator in Peking, P. Pierre Leroy, S.J., who is still an active member of the *Union des Croyants* today.

8. C. Cuénot, *Teilhard de Chardin*, p. 297.

9. Ibid., p. 298.

10. For a discussion of this essay, see chapter 9, "Teilhard's Comparison of Western and Eastern Mysticism," in this book.

11. Contributions 1-6 are listed in C. Cuénot's bibliography except for contribution 2. They are found under numbers 265, 286, 298, 303, and 304. Contribution 1 (no. 265) is acknowledged as addressed to "World Congress of Faiths, Branche française, Musée Guimet." Contribution 5 (no. 303) has a self-evident title, "Le Congrès Universel des Croyants." No other acknowledgment to the World Congress of Faiths is made in the listed bibliography, although vol. vii and its English translation, *Activation of Energy*, acknowledge this address for contribution 6 by adding "Written on the occasion of a lecture given, for the *Congrès Universel des Croyants*, at the home of M. de Saint-Martin . . ." Cf. *Activation of Energy*, p. 243. Here lies perhaps part of the reason for the omission. Only contribution 1 represents an essay written for a public lecture, while contributions 3, 4, and 6 are listed as *causeries* (talks) in the history of the French branch; i.e., they were talks given at the homes of members of the World Congress of Faiths in Paris.

12. P. Teilhard de Chardin, *The Future of Man* (London: Collins, 1965), p. 185.

13. Ibid., pp. 189, 190, and 192. My own translation from the French original as the published English translation is not always accurate.

14. *Le Congrès Universel des Croyants – Historique – 1946-1962*, p. 2.

15. P. Teilhard de Chardin, *Science and Christ* (London: Collins, 1968), pp. 197-98.

16. *Future of Man*, p. 76.

17. Ibid., p. 81.

18. *Writings in Time of War*, p. 14.

19. This has been confirmed by one of the former general secretaries; cf.

also Cuénot's remark, *Teilhard de Chardin*, p. 296.

20. Cyclostyled text of discussion, p. 38. An extract is quoted in chapter 5 (see p. 92 above).

21. P. Teilhard de Chardin, *Activation of Energy* (London: Collins, 1970), pp. 192 f. and 194 f. Cuénot, *Teilhard de Chardin*, p. 297, mentions that Teilhard discussed the subject of "existential fear" with Grousset in January 1949 and the day afterwards, he lent a copy of the essay to Madame S. Lemaître. There is no mention of the essay being written for the World Congress of Faiths, in whose historical survey the subject appears as the title of the talk of January 29, 1949 (on p. 14). J. Bacot, "Quelques Evocations," p. 148, similarly mentions that this talk was given to the World Congress of Faiths and that Gabriel Marcel was present when Teilhard spoke about "existential fear." About the divergent views of the two thinkers, see their debate about "Science and Consciousness" in January 1947, C. Cuénot, *Teilhard de Chardin*, pp. 251 f. Several references to existentialist thought can also be found in Teilhard's diary of that time.

22. *Future of Man*, pp. 287 f.

23. *Activation of Energy*, p. 238.

24. For a discussion of Teilhard's image of God see my article "The Death of God — the Rebirth of God': A Study in the Thought of Teilhard de Chardin," *The Modern Churchman* 18, 1974, pp. 46-51.

25. *Activation of Energy*, pp. 241 f.; my translation.

26. Ibid., p. 242.

In order to judge further influences of the association with the World Congress of Faiths in Teilhard's work, it is necessary to look at Teilhard's correspondence with Madame S. Lemaître (unpublished so far). There is also evidence of Teilhard's discussions with Swami Siddheswarananda from the Ramakrishna-Mission, one of the council members at that time. Teilhard probably refers to him indirectly in some of his essays and letters dating from this period.

27. See chapter 4 of my book *Towards A New Mysticism: Teilhard de Chardin and Eastern Religions* (London: Collins and New York: Seabury Press, 1980).

*Chapter 9*

1. P. Teilhard de Chardin, *Christianity and Evolution* (London: Collins, 1971), p. 122.

2. P. Teilhard de Chardin, *Toward the Future* (London: Collins, 1975). I have mostly used my own translations based on the French original, *Les Directions de l'Avenir* (Paris: Editions du Seuil, 1973).

3. *Toward the Future*, pp. 40-59.

4. Ibid., pp. 134-47.

5. See U. King, *Towards A New Mysticism: Teilhard de Chardin and Eastern Religions* (London: Collins and New York: Seabury Press, 1980).

6. *Toward the Future*, p. 42.

7. Ibid., p. 45.

Siddheswarananda from the Ramakrishna Mission, who had explained to him the different kinds of yogas and confirmed that the highest ecstasy corresponded in India to the definite loss of consciousness in an impersonal All. So Teilhard asked in a note in *Toward the Future*, p. 139, whether bhakti yoga, or the mysticism of love, is not basically of the "Western" type and therefore irreducible to the original and authentic intentions of Vedanta.

25. *Toward the Future*, p. 145.

26. In P. Teilhard de Chardin, *The Activation of Energy* (London: Collins, 1970), pp. 215-27.

27. Cf. R.C. Zaehner, *Evolution in Religion: A Study in Sri Aurobindo and P.T. de Chardin* (Oxford: Clarendon Press, 1971); cf. also R.C. Zaehner, "Teilhard and Eastern Religions" in *The Teilhard Review* 2 (1967-68), pp. 41-53.

28. *Toward the Future*, pp. 209-11.

29. *Activation of Energy*, p. 215.

30. See the letter quoted in note 17 above.

31. My italics. Cf. R. Robertson, *The Sociological Interpretation of Religion* (Oxford: Blackwell, 1970) p. 90.

32. F.C. Happold, *Mysticism: A Study and Anthology* (Harmondsworth: Penguin Books, 1971), p. 395.

33. *Evolution and Religion*, p. 7.

34. H. de Lubac, *Lettres Intimes*, p. 150. For Monchanin's thought about India, see his papers *Mystique de L'Inde Mystère Chrétien*, ed. Suzanne Siauve (Paris: Fayard, 1974).

35. See Maria-Ina Bergeron, *La Chine et Teilhard* (Paris: Jean Pierre Delarge, 1976); also Allerd Stikker, *A Comparison of Some Major Aspects of Western Thought, Taoist Philosophy and Teilhard de Chardin*, M.A. dissertation, University of Leeds, 1986.

36. Quoted by C.A. Moore in H. Chaudhuri and F. Spiegelberg, eds., *The Integral Philosophy of Aurobindo* (London: George Allen and Unwin, 1960), p. 94. A comprehensive study of the theme of evolution in the two thinkers is found in J. Feys, *Evolution in Aurobindo and Teilhard* (Calcutta: Mukhopadhyay, 1973). Convergent lines of thought between Teilhard and Eastern religions are explored by B. Bruteau, *Evolution Toward Divinity — T. de Chardin and the Hindu Traditions* (Wheaton, Ill.: The Theosophical Publishing House, 1974).

37. C. Cuénot, *Teilhard de Chardin*, p. 10.

*Chapter 10*

1. This chapter is a revised version of the Annual Memorial Lecture given to the Sri Aurobindo Society of Great Britain in December 1971 and later printed in *The Teilhard Review* 9 (1974), pp. 2-5.

2. R.C. Zaehner, *Evolution in Religion: A Study in Teilhard de Chardin and Sri Aurobindo* (Oxford: Clarendon Press, 1971). Ninian Smart compared Aurobindo's ideas with Teilhard's *Phenomenon of Man* as early as 1961; earlier comparisons exist, however, notably in French and German. The earliest

8. Ibid., p. 46.

9. Ibid., pp. 48, 49.

10. Ibid., p. 53.

11. Ibid., p. 43. Ever since he had begun to write, Teilhard tried to preser a philosophical solution to the problem of the One and the Many; see the important essay "Creative Union" in his book *Writings in Time of War* (London: Collins, 1968), and the study by D. Gray, *The One and the Many: Teilhard de Chardin's Vision of Unity* (London: Burns and Oates, 1969).

12. He first went to India in 1935.

13. P. Johanns, *Vers le Christ par le Vedanta*, 2 vols. (Louvain: Museum Lessianum 13, 1932).

14. The *Carnet de Lecture* is available only in manuscript form at the Fondation Teilhard de Chardin in Paris. The notes on Johanns's book *To Christ through the Vedanta* are analyzed in U. King, *Towards A New Mysticism*, pp. 241-47 (see note 5 above).

15. H. de Lubac, *Images de l'Abbé Monchanin* (Paris: Aubier Montaigne, 1967), pp. 121 and 123.

16. H. de Lubac, *Lettres Intimes de Teilhard de Chardin à Auguste Valensin, Bruno de Solages, Henri de Lubac* (Paris: Aubier Montaigne, 1972), p. 246. The translation of this text is found in C. Cuénot, *Teilhard de Chardin — A Biographical Study* (London: Burns and Oates, 1965), p. 142.

17. Ibid.; cf. *Lettres Intimes*, p. 269.

18. C. Cuénot, *Ce que Teilhard a vraiment dit* (Paris: Stock, 1972), p. 224.

19. Ibid., pp. 226 f. His letter of April 29, 1934 (quoted in note 17 above) seems to indicate, however, that he did not take the distinction between the Void and the Ineffable as perhaps only a difference of words. He wrote in the same letter: "I know that fully-achieved being can be called non-being. But I do not believe that there is, in the case in question, no more than a question of words." Cuénot, *Ce que Teilhard a vraiment dit*, p. 142.

20. In *Revue de la Pensée Juive 5 (1950*, pp. 105-13.

21. The stereotype about Eastern spirituality and Western materialism is found in the writings of many Hindu reformers and today also in the literature of neo-Hindu missionary movements. See U. King, *Indian Spirituality, Western Materialism: An Image and its Function in the Reinterpretation of Modern Hinduism* (New Delhi: Indian Social Institute, 1985).

22. *Toward the Future*, p. 135.

23. The attraction and strength of this organic naturalism of China has often been emphasized in the writings of J. Needham. Cf. his essay "The Past in China's Present" in *Within the Four Seas — the Dialogue of East and West* (London: George Allen and Unwin, 1969), pp. 30-88. In a footnote on p. 67 he writes: "The most recent world picture in this tradition, drawn, however, neither by a professional philosopher nor by a Marxist theoretician, but by a brilliant and unorthodox Jesuit, is *The Phenomenon of Man* by T. de Chardin."

24. These and other passages show that Teilhard equated Indian spirituality largely with Vedanta monism. Teilhard had encountered Swami

comparison ever to be made may well be the note, probably dating from 1956, left among the unpublished papers of P. Monchanin, who lived in South India at the time. Smart's article has been reprinted in *Sri Aurobindo 1872-1972 — Herald and Pioneer of Future Man, A Centenary Symposium*, Sri Aurobindo Society of Great Britain, 1973, pp. 15-22. I have briefly compared Aurobindo's and Teilhard's notion of evolution in my book *Towards A New Mysticism: Teilhard de Chardin and Eastern Religions* (London: Collins and New York: Seabury Press, 1980); see the chapter on "Religion and Evolution," especially section IV, pp. 183-86. One of the most recent comparisons, written from a predominantly Aurobindian perspective, is K.D. Sethna, *The Spirituality of the Future: A Search Apropos of R.C. Zaehner's Study on Sri Aurobindo and Teilhard de Chardin* (London and Toronto: Associated University Presses, 1981).

3. A Monestier, *Teilhard et Sri Aurobindo*, Carnet Teilhard 10 (Paris: Editions Universitaries, 1963), p. 6.

4. Most quotations from Aurobindo's works are taken from the anthology *The Future Evolution of Man — The Divine Life Upon Earth* compiled by P.B. Saint-Hilaire (Pondicherry: Sri Aurobindo Ashram, 1963). Ibid., p. 29.

5. Sri Aurobindo, *The Human Cycle* (Pondicherry: Sri Aurobindo Ashram, 1949), p. 327.

6. *The Future Evolution of Man*, p. 51.

7. Ibid., p. 55.

8. Cf. ibid., p. 41.

9. P. Teilhard de Chardin, *The Future of Man* (London: Collins, 1965), pp. 122 f.

10. Sri Aurobindo, *The Mind of Light*, ed. R.A. McDermott (New York: Dutton and Co., 1971).

11. Ibid., p. 85.

12. For a more detailed discussion, see the earlier chapter "Socialization and the Future of Humankind" in this book, pp. 29-43.

13. K.D. Sethna, *The Vision and Work of Aurobindo* (Pondicherry: Aurobindo Ashram, 1968), p. vii; see also Sethna's study quoted in note 2.

*Conclusion:*

1. Brian Swimme, *The Universe Is A Green Dragon: A Cosmic Creation Story* (Santa Fe: Bear & Company, 1984).

2. P. Teilhard de Chardin, *The Phenomenon of Man* (London: Collins, 1966), p. 295.

3. P. Teilhard de Chardin, *Human Energy*, p. 72.

4. _____, *Writings in Time of War*, pp. 117, 118, and 120.

5. _____, *Letters to Léontine Zanta* (London: Collins, 1969), p. 71 f.

6. _____, *Future of Man*, pp. 54 f.

7. _____, *Human Energy*, pp. 33 f., p.34.

8. Ibid., p. 78.

9. Henri de Lubac, *The Eternal Feminine: A Study of the Text of Teilhard de Chardin* (London: Collins, 1971).

10. P. Teilhard de Chardin, *Heart of Matter*, pp. 59 f.

11. _____, *Phenonemon of Man*, pp. 295 f.

12. The integration of these perspectives in Teilhard's thought was highlighted in some of the publications which appeared for the centenary of his death; see Jerome Perlinski, ed., *The Spirit of the Earth: A Teilhard Centennial Celebration* (New York: The Seabury Press, 1981); Sister Margaret McGurn, I.H.M., *Global Spirituality: Planetary Consciousness in the Thought of Teilhard de Chardin and Robert Muller* (Ardsley-on-Hudson, N.Y.: World Happiness and Cooperation, 1981); Thomas M. King, S.J. and James F. Salmon, S.J., eds., *Teilhard and the Unity of Knowledge* (New York: Paulist Press, 1983).

13. See R. Muller, "My Five Teilhardian Enlightenments" in J. Perlinski, *Spirit of Earth*, also in R. Muller, *New Genesis: Shaping A Global Spirituality* (New York: Doubleday, 1982), pp. 159-68.